ASBURY LANE

JULIE NEVEL

SHINEWORTHY PUBLISHING

NASHVILLE | TENNESSEE

SHINEWORTHY PUBLISHING
NASHVILLE | TENNESSEE

Asbury Lane by Julie Nevel

Copyright © 2016 by Shineworthy Publishing, Nashville, Tennessee

Request for information should be addressed to sueann@shineworthy.com

Printed in the United States of America

First Printing, 2016

ISBN-10:0-9981664-0-5

ISBN-13:978-0-9981664-0-7

Shineworthy Publishing

Positive Life Books

257 Clear Lake Drive West

Nashville, TN 37217

To the best of the author's knowledge and belief, all statements of fact contained in the work are true and based on appropriate and diligent research.

Cover and Interior Layout & Design by Becky Bayne, Becky's Graphic Design

ASBURY LANE

VERSE 1

I grew up on a farm at the end of a lane
Where living and loving were one and the same
Adventures were many, sorrows were few
As kids we could always find something to do

We'd explore in the barn and play ball in the fields
Skate on the pond and we'd sled down the hills
We'd go to our tree house whenever we could
We had our own little world in the woods

The lane was adorned with wild flowers and trees
I've never found better treasures than these
And the bittersweet wild cherries, on Asbury Lane
Asbury Lane, Asbury Lane

CHORUS

Where we learned to love Jesus and we learned to love life
It never occurred to me that I should ask why
I just knew that I loved livin' on Asbury Lane

VERSE 2

The older I grew the more keenly aware
I became of God's presence surrounding me there
Our home was a warm place, a haven for friends
A good cup of tea just before the day's end

A song 'round the piano, a dinner time prayer
Church ev'ry Sunday and good times to share
I loved to wander the hills by myself
And put into writing the things that I felt

I never thought I would leave there one day
But grown-up things found me and called me away
And I took with me sweet memories of Asbury Lane
Asbury Lane, Asbury Lane

BRIDGE 1

In the summer a canopy of green leaves
When the snow flies a winter wonderland
In the autumn the colored leaves dance in the wind
In the spring it all blossoms again
On Asbury Lane, Asbury Lane

CHORUS

Where we learned to love Jesus and we learned to love life
It never occurred to me that I should ask why
I just knew that I loved livin' on Asbury Lane

VERSE 3

I love to go back to the farm when I can
Hike up the hill and look over the land
Take walks and tell stories to my sisters' kids
Now they're doing all of the things that we did

Everyone has their own story to tell
I've had my triumphs and my struggles as well
I'm thankful for parents who gave roots and wings
I thank God for life and a reason to sing

I've found my own way and a few of my dreams
But no place can stir my soul better it seems

Than where I found fresh strawberries on Asbury Lane
Asbury Lane, Asbury Lane

BRIDGE 2

Now the barn doesn't seem quite so mysterious
And the path in the woods is not so long
But the love and the values that shaped who I am
Still surround me and my heart belongs
On Asbury Lane, Asbury Lane

CHORUS

Where we learned to love Jesus and we learned to love life
Blessings were countless like stars in the sky
And I still love to walk there on Asbury Lane

Where we learned to love Jesus and we learned to love life
This side of heaven there's nothing as nice
As a day pickin' raspberries on Asbury Lane
Asbury Lane, Asbury Lane

Words & music by Julie Nevel
© Nevel Music

PROLOGUE

There is a beautiful place of sanctuary at the end of a road named Asbury Lane, a 100-acre farm in the rolling hills of central Pennsylvania where I was blessed to be raised on a strong foundation of love, faith, and family. Throughout my life, I have tried to share this special place by bringing people "home" to experience it, writing songs about it, hosting retreats there, and recounting memories and stories with my parents, four siblings, many cousins and friends. I realize it is a rare thing in today's transient world to grow up in one place with family intact! I didn't know any different when I was a child, thus the line "it never occurred to me that I should ask why." As an adult, I've come to realize perhaps I should ask why. Why and how did my parents, Paul and Betty Nevel, find each other, begin a family, and come to live on a farm? I knew some of their story, but I began to dig deeper and ask a lot of questions. How did they as newlyweds navigate being separated by war when dad was drafted by the Army? What were the trials and joys of raising a family in the 1960s and 70s? Why did they move to Asbury Lane, what were their dreams and how were they prepared to take care of a farm and raise a family? What was our experience as their children, and what was it about this place that was so special and that still draws me back home?

I've come to realize there is much more to be told than what a song can contain, thus the purpose for this book! My desire as I write this story is to honor God and my parents who gave us roots and wings, and the gift of an amazing legacy. As with any novel based on a true story, in order to fill in the gaps, I've had to let my imagination soar where memories have waned. My hope is to convey to you, the reader, the spirit of a place of love and grace, and to allow you to experience it, too. I welcome you to come away with me to my little corner of the world that I still call home, years after moving away. Take a walk down the lane, meet some interesting characters, discover fun adventures in the woods, borrow a tradition to make your own, lay back in a freshly cut hay field under a starry summer night, and let your senses and imagination be filled with the sights and sounds of creation exalting its Creator! As you read and journey with me, may the blessing personally be yours.

Julie Nevel, 2016

DEDICATION

I dedicate this book to my precious Gram "Betty" Myers, who passed on to me, among many wonderful things, a love for words and books. I also dedicate this writing to my amazing parents Paul and Betty Nevel, with eternal appreciation for their unconditional love and living legacy, and to my family and all those who have gone before us and paved the way to Asbury Lane.

ACKNOWLEDGMENTS

Though I have written songs for many years, my mother has been telling me for a while now that I needed to write a book. She envisioned it to be about my travels, adventures and God-stories along the way; a book about me, not about her. However, I have been reminding her that this saga started with her and Dad! Those other stories will be written, but my parents' story is where it all began. Therefore, many thanks go to Mom for planting the seed that grew and led me to become an author, and to Dad for following his dream that led us all to Asbury Lane. Writing my first book has certainly been a challenge, a joy, a struggle, a learning process, and ultimately a wonderful experience. I've laughed and cried, stared at a blank screen, worked many a night into the wee hours of morning, asked my parents a million questions, and spent many hours researching (thank the Lord for the internet!) and looking at old home movies and hundreds of pictures. At times I felt I was slowly wading through stagnant marshes until I finally reached fresh waters of words that flowed freely. I am so thankful to many who were a part of the process, from those who were hands-on to those who aided in sharing memories and who cheered me on!

I am indebted and very grateful to my publisher and literary mentor Sue Ann Cordell, who had the vision for the content of this book before I did and who has seen me through from conception to completion. "Trust and write, Julie Sue, just trust and write," were words I heard often from her. I certainly needed deadlines and accountability to keep me on track! She has given so much of her time to see this come to fruition. Her belief in me and the project, as well as her prayers, have spurred me on to the finish line.

It might go without saying, but I can't possibly go without saying a big thank you to my siblings Bonnie Hamer, Gail Hamilton, Karen Kennedy, Jay Nevel, and their families for their support and trust in me to write our family's story. I needed their memories and prayers as well! I was, and continue to be, inspired by my nieces, nephews, great nieces and great nephews for whom and through whom we pray the legacy will continue. I love you all so very much!

The Rudasill gang, my aunts, uncles, cousins, extended family and many friends played important roles in this narrative. The Ardreys, Hardings, Nevels, Sengs and Sharffs have been integral parts of our backstory and I love how God has weaved our lives together. I asked Joyce (Ardrey) Acker, Pennie (Harding) Cadwallader, Judy Harding, Patty Nevel, Harry Sharff and others to reminisce and share their thoughts and they graciously obliged. I missed not being able to talk to my cousin David Ardrey, as he passed from this life too soon yet is so much a part of my early memories. Lifelong friends Lori (Pitonyak) Trautman and Cathy (Shaver) Reightler were a huge help as they shared their recollections and cheered me on! I am indebted to best of friends Shelly Lappi and Colleen McCallus, who daily saw my ups and downs, listened and encouraged me to keep at it. Many thanks go to the Barrentines for Nashville housing, Carol A., Shirley C., Sarah H., Bon K., Connie M., Mary P., Vic P., Julie P., Dawn Y., Jan Z., my Super 7 family, Tess Hamel, and Nevel Music assistant, Kristy Steppe for precious friendship and prayers. I am grateful to Nikki Brungard, true friend and grammar queen, who freely offered assistance. I thank the Lord for my dear friend and mentor Betty Gray, who introduced me to Sue Ann and encouraged me along the way. I deeply appreciate each one of my "Friends in Faith" partners who have celebrated the journey with me and prayed faithfully over this book.

Many thanks go to the talented, techy, artsy and creative Becky Bayne for the book's layout and design, as well as for her prayers! I also want to give a shout out to my nephew Josh Hamer for offering his time and creativity to the design ideas. I thank Richard Black for joining the team with his expertise as an author and freelance writer. I am grateful to those behind the scenes who, as part of Sue Ann's Asbury Lane team in Nashville, read, critiqued, and offered professional advice.

Above all, I give all the glory and my deepest gratitude to God who is the giver of all good gifts and gave me His amazing grace, a precious family, a beautiful place to call home, and a story to write.

ASBURY LANE

JULIE NEVEL

ONE

To write about a great love story, a magnificent love story of epic proportions, is not difficult. It is there for all to see, visible and often simple in the telling. And yet, the most wonderful of love stories are those that happen around us; sweet and beautiful, they can be found everywhere but often go unnoticed by their very nature. This is such a love story; innocent in an age of innocence, an anchor at a time when the world was changing and resilient when impermanence was becoming the norm.

Even though the two souls who would create the miracle love story of Asbury Lane were born and raised mere miles from each other, they did not initially know of each other and would not wonderfully, magically meet for nineteen years. Nevertheless, they came into the world in similar fashion and grew up in typical families of their age. Their first years of life prepared them to come together for a lifetime of love and affection.

For America, it was the time between wars, though no one yet knew it. The First World War was called the war to end all wars because of the horrors and death it brought to Europe and the scale of war visited around the world. The generation that lived through it could not imagine another war would ever be fought. They were wrong. The foolishness of the world following World War I set the stage for the Second World War.

But in Altoona, Pennsylvania, while the world was stumbling toward conflict, peace and life went undisturbed by the global events building in Europe. The train had made travel easier and faster for residents of the town. It also brought jobs as most of the industrial workers of the area worked for the railroad in one capacity or another. Sound had come to movies and Hollywood was peddling confidence, optimism and diversion to a public weary of the drudgery of the Great Depression. It was the beginning of the Swing Era of music and the big bands. They dominated the music and film industries as movies and phonograph records brought entertainment to every community. The Ford Model T had come on the scene soon after the turn of the century and motor vehicles were becoming affordable and accessible to everyone.

The world outside of Altoona was speeding up but on February 25, 1932 everyone in the Nevel house was focused on one event.

It was a very long day for James and Murry Nevel, especially Murry.

Birthing a baby at that time often took place at home. It was difficult and a little dangerous; it was women's work and the responsibility of trained doctors. Therefore, men were expected to stay out of the way. Consequently, James had been pacing circles in the living room with sweat on his brow and his heart pounding in worry and dread; man's work. Murry's brother, Paul, was at his side, trying to lighten the mood by teasing him and telling him he looked like he was the one in labor instead of his wife.

Finally, the doctor descended the stairs and announced, "It's a boy!"

When James heard the news, all six feet of his narrow frame melted into a puddle on the floor.

"A boy, Pauly, a boy, it's a boy! Oh my gosh, good golly, I'm a dad!" He turned to the general practitioner, "Doc, is my wife okay? Are they both okay? Can I see them now?"

Dr. Donovan smiled as he reached out his hand to congratulate James. "Here, let me help you up. Yes, Mother and baby are both doing well, and they are waiting to see you."

"I'll wait down here, my good brother," Paul offered. "Go upstairs and see your wife and baby boy."

James was getting his legs back and took three steps at a time. When he was almost to the top of the staircase, he slowed his pace and turned around. "We're naming him after you, Pauly. You've been here for us through this whole thing. How could we name him anything else?"

Paul looked surprised and blushed. "No, really? Well you might have to find out what my sister has to say about that, first."

James winked at him. "It was her idea."

As he opened the door to the bedroom and entered, James heard Paul shouting downstairs, "Oh my gosh, good golly. I'm an uncle!"

Meanwhile, James took a deep breath, stood up straight and dignified and walked over to Murry. He leaned over and kissed his wife on the forehead. "Murry, are you okay? I know you went through a lot up here while I was doing nothing but pacing and praying downstairs. I'm sorry you had to…"

"Look at him, James." Murry shushed him by holding out their new son. "He's here. He's so perfect, so worth it all."

James sat down gingerly on the bed beside his wife and looked closer at the little face peering out of the small yellow baby blanket while Murry cuddled him in her arms. "Do you want to hold him, James?"

He sighed and wiped a tear from his cheek. It was such an unmanly thing to do, allowing the emotion to show, but this was a special exception. "Yes, maybe, but, well I'm not sure. He is so tiny."

"You'll be just fine. Don't worry, dear." Murry winced as she made the effort to lift him toward James. "Here, easy, hold your hand behind his little head like this."

Seeing his wife's struggle, James quickly reached out and took the little bundle. "Murry, honey, take it easy I've got him."

The new mother leaned back, relaxed and watched her husband cradle their new baby boy. Life could not get much better for the couple.

The new father's emotions were soaring as he remembered back to the day when Murry told him she was going to have a baby. They were having a baby.

It was eight months ago, but seemed so long ago now. "You're what? What are you? You're pregnant?" James practically yelled as he put his hands to his head in disbelief. "Are you sure?"

His reaction did not completely take her by surprise; she thought he might not be pleased with the news. She looked down at her flat stomach. Nothing externally had changed but she thought she could feel changes inside. "Yes, I'm sure."

"But we have barely had time to get used to one another, let alone bring a child into the marriage." He shook his head. His mind was spinning with panic, doubt, joy, fear. "And I just got laid off. How are we going to afford this, Murry?"

She started to cry. "Well, it's not all my fault. You know what caused this and you haven't exactly been avoiding it! Quite the opposite, in fact, every day and night since our wedding!"

Slightly embarrassed, he softened and sat down beside her. "Okay, you're right, but you are irresistible."

She blushed. It was the type of conversation that was rarely spoken even in private. And they were young, inexperienced in expressing their love.

He continued, "I'm sorry. It's just that, well, it comes as quite a shock. I didn't expect us to have a child this quickly. It's only been a month since our wedding. I guess it's a honeymoon baby? I don't know if I'm ready. Are you? Are we?"

Murry sighed and put her hand on his. "Well, I suppose we have about eight months to get ready."

But now with his son in his arms, James thought about how the past eight months had crawled by, most of it in the cold and snow of the relentless winter of 1931 going into 1932. He was able to get part-time work at the railroad. An inexperienced father-to-be, he barely let his wife out of the house for fear that she might fall on the ice. The couple was living with her parents so thankfully, there were others around to care for Murry when James was away at work. Being one of the fifteen children of the Rudasill clan, Murry kept busy and when funds allowed, there was always a dress to sew, a meal to cook or a cake to bake.

The family came together on the big day. Murry's mother and sisters tended to her through agonizing labor, while he paced the floor, downstairs with the men.

Looking at the precious little bundle he held so carefully, James could hardly believe after the months of worry, stress and anticipation that their baby had really arrived. Oh, he checked without Murry noticing what he was doing. Yes, ten fingers, ten toes; a healthy, normal child.

Suddenly he did not feel so worried anymore. "My son. Our son. We're gonna be okay. Your daddy's here, little fella." He felt the heavy weight of responsibility balanced by an almost giddy relief. "You're going to be proud to wear your uncle's name and I hope to make you proud to wear your daddy's name too. Paul James Nevel, welcome to the world."

Years passed and little Paul was growing up too quickly for the likes of his mother. He seemed slow to start walking, but once he caught on, it seemed he never slowed down. He was a quick learner and had an early interest in trains and building blocks. He liked to sing and found he had a pretty good voice people appreciated listening to; at least that was what the church choir director said. By the time Paul was 10 years old, he had three siblings, Jake, Myra Sue and Tommy. Sadly, there was also little Jacqueline who was stillborn but loved just the same, though she belonged to God. Paul was a big help around the house and loved being a big brother.

When Paul was in Junior High School, he joined the band. His mother always liked the saxophone and, since she encouraged him to take up an instrument, he wanted to learn how to play her instrument of choice. Unfortunately, saxophones were too expensive, and it was possible to buy a metal clarinet a lot cheaper. So Paul said he would give the clarinet a try. There was a private teacher who lived a mile away and Paul walked there for his lessons, proudly carrying his new clarinet in a black case. When he joined the band, he did not mind staying after school for practices since a number of his friends had also joined. Marching in parades and learning to count steps to perform the halftime shows on the field of the football games proved to be hard work and good exercise. It was especially arduous in the late summer and early fall when the days were hot. There were times when Paul wished he was the one playing football instead of only getting on the field to step in time with his clarinet, but he did not know if he had the talent to make the team. Besides, he was able to play with his neighborhood football team, which did not cost a cent and was lots of fun. It could be pretty rough at times without equipment and pads, as could happen when boys were allowed to be boys.

As with most rural Americans, Paul grew up going to church and remained involved even as a teenager. His social life revolved around church, school and, one of his favorite pastimes, roller skating. It was the teen activity of the period and he spent a considerable amount of time with his cousin, Glenn Ardrey, at Lakemont Park's Roller Skating Arena. They also went to movies at the local theatre and enjoyed gathering with friends at the drive-in diner, a new avenue for teens to meet that had not been available to their parents when they were that age.

Paul was keen on getting his license as soon as it was legal, as he had lots of experience driving tractors on his uncle's farm. His parents were able to help him get a car from someone they knew, making him the first and only teen in his neighborhood to own a vehicle. It was old and worn, but it was transportation! When the starter went bad, there was no money for repairs. Not to be discouraged, he came up with a clever way to get around the broken starter. He was careful to strategically park on a hill; lucky for him, hills were plentiful around Altoona! He would sit in the driver's seat, put the car in gear and push the clutch pedal all the way down. Then his brother Jake and a friend or two would push the car as they jogged alongside it. Once it hit a good enough speed, Paul would take his foot off the pedal, or "pop the clutch," the engine would start, the passengers would jump in, and away they would go!

All in all, for Paul Nevel, it was a quiet, simple and pleasant way to grow up in the world.

TWO

Eight and a half months after Paul entered the world, on November 10, 1932, another momentous event was happening not far away that would affect him later in life.

It was a long, grueling day for Sarah Elizabeth Myers. Called Betty by friends and family, those first pangs of labor necessitated a trip to the Altoona hospital and hours of emotional and physical struggle on the second floor in Labor and Delivery. Her husband, George Myers, known to all as Buck, was not allowed to see her after he dropped her off and the staff of the hospital whisked her away in a wheelchair. By the time he parked the car and returned, he discovered that his place was in the waiting room with all the other worried, anxious, expectant fathers. They all collectively proceeded to drive the nurses crazy with a persistent barrage of questions. "Is my wife okay? How long will this take? Has she had the baby yet? Are you sure she is okay? Do you think it will be a boy or a girl? Is everything going okay in there? Why is it taking so long?"

The staff was accustomed to nervous fathers and tried to reassure them and maintain an air of calm as best they could. However, as one-by-one the other men received the good news and left, Buck began to worry that something was very wrong. How could he know that birthing a baby was dependent entirely on the schedule of a little one who was about to consume, control and dominate his life? Therefore, he fretted and worried and thought about all that could possibly go wrong.

Buck was not the only one relieved when Dr. Donovan burst through the doors just four hours later exclaiming, "It's a girl!" The staff was very happy, indeed.

The new father felt the relief welling up inside and his eyes let go with unmanly tears to express it. He tried to let it sink in. "It's a girl? Are you sure, Doc?"

The doctor laughed out loud, "Uh, yes, it's pretty obvious, she's a girl alright." He shook Buck's hand. "Congratulations, Mr. Myers, you're a dad. You can go back and see your wife now. She is in room 202."

He was anxious as he went to find her room. It was not that he did not trust the doctor and nurses; he just wanted to see his wife for himself and know that everything was fine. When he opened the door to room 202, the first words out of Betty's mouth were, "Oh Bucky, I'm so glad you're here! I want to name her Elizabeth, after my middle name like we talked about. Elizabeth Louise is pretty. Do you like the sound of Elizabeth Louise?"

Truth be told, he would have agreed to anything at that moment knowing that his wife was healthy. "Sure, sweets, whatever you say. I don't mind it a bit. She might be called Lizzy though, or Beth or Betty."

"Oh no, I'd rather we stick with her given name. Can't we just tell people her name is Elizabeth, not some shortened version?"

He took her hands in his strong hands and looked into her tired eyes, savoring the knowledge that none of his worst fears had come to pass. "Well now, most folks call you Betty and it's not so bad for you, Betty," Buck said with a sideways smile and raised eyebrows.

He thought for a moment then playfully added, "I still don't know how people started calling you Betty when your name is Sarah Elizabeth."

It was her father's doing. He started calling her his "Little Bitty Betty" when she was a toddler and it stuck. Sometimes she was confused though, when the teacher in school called for Sarah and she was marked absent because she did not realize her name was being called.

"Well I sure hope she takes after you, sweets. If she gets her mother's looks and her dad's wit and smarts, she'll be quite a catch," he said with a wink.

"George Gaylord! Is that all I'm good for, my looks?" She always called him by his given name when he was in trouble. It was a joke between them, as she knew he would always talk her down and eventually make her laugh.

"Oh, you know better than that. Everyone knows you're really the brains of this outfit."

She chuckled then winced.

"Don't make me laugh, please, it hurts. I do hope she gets your musical talent. But for now, I just can't wait to hold her again. Do you think the nurse will be back soon?"

At just that moment, the door opened to Betty's hospital room and in walked two nurses. One was holding Buck and Betty's firstborn sweet little bundle wrapped in a soft pink blanket and the other came to check Betty's vitals and make sure she was still doing fine.

"How are you feeling, Mrs. Myers?" the one checking her pulse asked.

"Kind of weak and exhausted, but overall not too bad. I must say I am feeling much better than I was a little bit ago," Betty replied.

"Your wife was quite the trooper in there," the one with the new baby informed Buck. "Congratulations. Your little girl is beautiful and everything checked out just fine."

The couple sighed a collective sigh of relief.

The nurse gently placed the baby in Betty's arms. "Have you made a decision about her name yet? You'll have to sign papers soon and we'll need to know for the birth certificate."

"Can we have a moment please?" Betty asked.

It was the first opportunity she had to take a really good look at her newborn and examine her tiny features. Sound asleep, the baby could not have looked more angelic.

The nurses discreetly left the new family to privately discover each other.

"Oh Bucky, look at her. Who do you think she looks like? I can hardly believe she is here." There was no greater feeling than holding the baby in her arms. "After all these months and she's ours."

Buck walked around to her side and leaned over to kiss the baby's sweet rosy cheek. "Wow, just amazing. What a miracle," he whispered as his eyes glistened. He had never had such an overwhelming feeling like this before. It was like love and adoration, wonder, humility and responsibility all wrapped up in one breathtakingly tiny little package.

Betty ran her fingers across her precious one's little forehead. "I'm your mama and you are Elizabeth Louise. Yes, it suits you. Do you like your name, little one?"

The baby stirred and tried to open her eyes and Betty took that as a sign of approval. Buck thought so, too. "Elizabeth Louise it is, sweets."

Then the new father spoke softly to his daughter, "You'll be proud to wear your mother's middle name and to grow up a Myers like your daddy. Elizabeth Louise Myers, welcome to the world."

Elizabeth Louise Myers did, indeed, bring incredible joy to Buck and Betty. She was born to loving newlyweds who were just getting their feet wet with marriage and now they would add a baby to the mix. It was not uncommon for young couples to be young parents soon into their marriage.

Time quickly passed for Buck's very own little bitty Betty, an adorable sweet-cheeked, curly-haired toddler who captured attention everywhere she went. The name Betty stuck and that was that. Mother Betty was proud to take her everywhere and hear people talk about how adorable her daughter was. When little Betty was two years old, she became a big sister to Marlene Lorraine.

My sweet queen Marlene, her father called her.

The girls grew up not only sisters, but best friends. They had a lot of similar interests such as music and singing, which they did regularly in the church youth choir. They liked to roller skate and most Friday nights would go to the Jaffa Mosque Skating Rink in Altoona and spend hours circling the floor with their friends, swaying to the music. They often enjoyed Saturday afternoon movie matinees at the Lyric Theatre on Fourth Street; films of hope that the war would end in victory, stories of what was great about America and musicals with catchy tunes and beautiful people dancing.

Their dad, a painter by trade, had a creative side to him and loved music as well. Buck had a fascination with musical instruments from an early age and a keen ear for picking up melodies and chords to go with them. The 1930s saw the origination of the "jam session" in jazz and rock music as an informal gathering of musicians playing for their own pleasure. This gave a name to the spontaneous get-togethers Buck and his brother Joe often loved when friends and family would gather on Saturday evenings to sing popular favorite songs accompanied by the brothers on their guitars and banjos. Buck and Betty would walk the seven blocks mostly uphill to Buck's dad's house with girls in tow and spend the evening visiting and playing music on the front porch in the warmer months. The jam sessions moved into the living room during the cold Pennsylvania winter evenings. An added measure of excitement for the girls was when it snowed and their dad would let them take their sleds along. When it was time to return home, they slid down the hill to the house. As well as pickin' and grinnin' on the stringed instruments, Buck played the accordion. It took quite a good amount of coordination to push and pull the bellows while playing the buttons and keys with the left and right hands. He relished the challenge, but felt he needed help to improve his skills and proficiency, so he sent away to the United States School of Music for *48 Lessons for the Accordion*.

Encouraged by her father, Betty also worked through the lessons and developed a real appreciation for the accordion and it seemed to appreciate her. They were made for each other. She later found a private teacher around the time she graduated from high school and took a year of lessons, spending many hours practicing.

"I have a surprise for you," announced an excited Marlene. "The organizers of the softball league banquet want you to play!"

"Uh… play? They want me to play softball? I thought it was a men's league."

"No, silly! They want you to play the accordion at the banquet! You know, for the entertainment part of the evening. Isn't that great?"

Um, no, Betty did not consider that to be great. She played with her dad and uncle for their jam sessions and occasionally in church, but never really as a solo act in public. Gulp, no!

But what she said was, "Yeah, sure, well I guess so."

It was an honor to be asked, but she was as nervous as she was excited.

When Betty talked to her accordion teacher about helping her prepare, the older man was thrilled. "What a lovely opportunity for you. Don't you go doubting yourself, my dear. You are quite capable."

Together, they chose the music and prepared Betty for the performance.

She practiced for hours and worried for more hours. She imagined all of the embarrassing things that could go wrong. However, never in her wildest dreams did she imagine the most wonderful, absolutely fabulous thing that could happen.

THREE

As Paul Nevel and Betty Myers grew, almost neighbors but never meeting as children, so did America. They came of age in the 1940s, the turbulent years of World War II and the uneasy peace that followed when the world was divided into East and West, freedom and communism. It was a black and white world of liberty against bondage.

Bing Crosby, Frank Sinatra, Perry Como, Ella Fitzgerald and Louis Armstrong dominated the music scene. It was the height of the Hollywood movie studio system which turned out films like factories made cars and other mass-produced products for a public that went to the theater once or twice a week. The demographic formerly known as adolescents began to be called "teenagers." The automobile gave teenagers more freedom to socialize along with the growth of the soda shops and inclusion of jukeboxes to play their favorite music on demand.

At Altoona Area High School in 1950, Paul and Betty were finishing their senior years still unaware that the other person existed. Out of over 700 graduating students, their senior pictures in their yearbook, the Horseshoe, were just a page apart. They graduated in the same class on the same day with both their families and friends watching and yet, they were complete strangers.

During the same time, a new regional military conflict sprouted up. Initial reports of the successes in the far-off remote corner of the world called Korea spawned celebrations in the United States and many Western nations. The newly-formed United Nations sent troops which included Americans but few at home understood why or what was happening. There was hope of a quick resolution to whatever caused the hostilities and for a rapid return home of the troops. Then the Red Army of Communist China entered the conflict in defense of the North Korean People's Army, pouring across the border between the two countries in great numbers. What had appeared to be a United Nations victory escalated into a war they were losing. The radio and newspaper headlines stopped talking about the imminent end of the fighting. Begun as some kind of a military police action to keep communist North Korea in check and the free Republic of South Korea from being overrun, it had turned into a full-blown shooting war.

Americans were trying to get back on their feet after the devastation of two World Wars and the Great Depression. Many had no desire to enter yet another conflict perpetrated by the East/West divisions the end of the war created which politicians referred to as the Cold War. What was to become known as the Korean War did not have the same impact on the people back home in the States as had the two World Wars. The overall morale across the country was more peaceful and positive. The supply and demand for goods and services created by the previous war brought the country out of the Great Depression and the economy was on a steady rise with the constant creation of new products and services to buy. There were cars in most driveways and drive-in diners in most towns where people, and especially teenagers, would drive to eat instead of eating at home. Houses were becoming increasingly available to the average family and new neighborhoods were built. The American people wanted to enjoy the fruits of their economic success, not engage in more wars.

With the coming of the summer of 1951, all was peaceful in the railroad town in the Northeast of the United States known as Altoona, Pennsylvania.

Nevertheless, the chance of a prolonged military conflict concerned young men like Paul Nevel and his cousin Glenn. The draft instituted during the last war was kept in place to fill the ranks of each branch of the military. The United States was a world power with armed forces scattered across the world and the manpower requirements to maintain a global military presence.

Paul tried to stay abreast of world events beyond his community and state, yet reports of ongoing war and the need for more troops was sobering news he did not want to hear. He and his friends knew they were susceptible to be called into military service should the war persist.

"Surely not, it's not our country's problem," he would tell himself. "Please, God, not us, not me," he would pray. It was not cowardice nor was he self-centered. He was a young Christian man of peace who did not want to fight in a war.

Meanwhile for both Paul and Betty, life took an unexpected turn on September 19, 1951 when their lives finally intersected. As love stories go, it was one filled with the fairy tale elements that would rival even the best teller of fantasy stories and contained a romantic twist. And as happened in those stories, this one came during a simple moment while two people were living everyday life with their friends and neighbors.

"Wonderful meal, as usual!" Paul remarked to Glenn as he pushed his chair back from the table to get comfortable for the evening's entertainment. Glenn patted his full belly as he smiled a silly grin and nodded in agreement. Their slow-paced world was one of simple pleasures where family, friendships and community were important. The two of them were more like brothers than cousins and participated in a variety of activities together; playing softball and football, roller skating, a night on the porch in the soft summer air swapping stories and occasional social events such as church dinners and banquets.

Paul had grown into a handsome nineteen-year-old with short, neatly trimmed dark hair and glasses, a fit and strong physique, still wearing a suntan from working outside on his Uncle Ken's farm during the summer.

Just two weeks younger than Paul, Glenn had a fair complexion dotted with freckles, light blonde hair, a thin body with a narrow face, accented by a big nose that he would quip about before anyone else had the chance. He was quick with a joke and had a charismatic personality that made everyone he met feel like he was their friend.

They were attending the annual September end-of-season banquet for the Altoona citywide church softball league. Second Avenue Evangelical United Brethren Church was the perfect venue for banquets and special occasions, because the building included a large room for social events, complete with a stage. Both of the young men had grown up going to church with their families at the First Church of Christ, several blocks over on 6th Avenue and 9th Street. The program began, as it always did, with awards being distributed amidst lots of cheering, some good-natured jeering and applauding. Then there was music, which proved to be an unexpected and interesting addition to the evening. A pretty young lady introduced as Betty

Myers walked onto the stage with her accordion to the warm greeting by the audience. As she began to play, everything around Paul lost its focus and all he could see and hear was her.

Much has been said or fantasized about love at first sight. Some would say that it is nonexistent, others that it only happens in fairy tales or the movies. But in the social hall of the Second Avenue E.U.B. Church that night, the seeds of love were planted in the heart of Paul Nevel.

A lover of music, Paul was drawn to Betty's talent and then mesmerized by her beauty. The music and the good looks merged into one and he could not look away from her. Though if he closed his eyes at that moment, he was certain he would still remember every one of her features and his ears would recognize her lovely music. Her dark curly hair fell to her shoulders, accenting her soft blue eyes and framing her lovely face and stunning smile. He was immediately taken by the sweet disposition she projected to match her slender, attractive figure.

"I want to meet that girl," he whispered in a daze.

"Did you say something?" asked a confused Glenn, glancing over. Then he caught a glimpse of the starry eyes and the captivated face and knew his cousin had been struck by something resembling love, or at least infatuation.

At the end of the evening, Paul quickly circulated around the room in hopes of casually running into the accordion player, but could not locate her anywhere among the people. He drifted over and hung around the stage where he thought those who were in the program would have emerged; no Betty Myers.

He could not know that, excited by the response to her performance, Betty had rushed home to tell the man she thought was her biggest fan, Buck. Had she known there was a bigger fan back in the Second Avenue E.U.B. Church social hall, she would not have left so soon.

In the meantime, Glenn finally caught up to his friend whom he had inexplicably lost.

"Where have you been?" he demanded.

In true macho fashion, Paul played it cool and casual, "Oh, thought I saw someone I knew."

Uh-huh, Glenn was not fooled. He had seen the expression on Paul's face and the puppy dog eyes glued to the pretty female musician. A joke came to mind but, uncharacteristically, he swallowed it. Sometimes, a guy just has to take one for his teammate.

That night, Paul lay on his bed, stared at the ceiling and wondered how he could find the girl with the accordion.

The enchanting music and lovely features of the musician consumed Paul's thoughts. For days after the banquet, he could not seem to get that beauty out of his mind. Would he ever see her again? How could he see her again? He really, really wanted to see her again.

How often the God of the Universe sees true love in the making and reaches out His hand to bless it might be a topic for theologians and angels, but in the small community of Altoona, there was a night in 1951 when God's hand was evident.

A couple of weeks had passed since the banquet and, unbeknownst to Paul, Betty Myers and her cousin Zada were off to the roller skating rink, as was their habit. It was one of their favorite activities, an inexpensive and popular hobby, not to mention good exercise. Some touted roller skating as America's number one participant sport at the time, providing wholesome family recreation, and keeping young people off the streets with this healthy, supervised alternative. Betty's father drove the two girls, intending to drop them off, but when they arrived at the Jaffa Mosque Skating Rink, they were disappointed to find it was closed that night due to repairs. They were young women who wanted to skate and socialize not return home for a quiet evening with the family, so they persuaded Buck to take them to the other rink in town. He agreed, knowing how much the girls looked forward to skating and he was not one for disappointing his little bitty Betty. As the girls climbed from the car, Buck told them to have fun and call for a ride home when they were done. Yet, it is not hard to imagine God, with a smile and a touch of His divine romantic nature, reaching out to sprinkle a little holy spiritual dust upon Lakemont Park's Roller Arena.

The Lakemont roller rink was brimming with an unusual number of skaters that evening. There was the usual crowd of regulars plus the overflow from the closed Jaffa rink. Standing patiently in line to buy tickets, Betty and Zada saw many of their friends who had also decided to make the drive across town. They could hear the organ music playing, inviting them with the promise of a night of fun and it did not matter that it would be packed, they were just glad to be there and could not wait to get inside.

Lakemont was the normal hangout for Paul and Glenn and they were already inside with their customary friends and acquaintances, as they were most Friday nights, delighting in the various skates to lively organ music. These types of social events allowed young people to meet and served as a safe place for couples to be introduced. Two people might skate a few rounds in casual conversation before daring to get closer in a couple skate with soft, romantic music, and even holding hands.

Glenn was taking a break to sit down and give his ankles a rest when he noticed more people streaming in and waiting in line at the check in counter. The buzz was that the Jaffa Mosque Skating Rink was closed which explained the larger than normal number of people. Then he did a double take when he saw a familiar face. He looked again, just to be sure. His tired ankles forgotten, he quickly darted back onto the floor to catch up to Paul who had just glided by with their friends.

"Paul, wait up!" He skated toward his cousin and friend like a man with a secret that had to get out.

Paul looked back and slowed down for Glenn to move up beside him.

"Guess who just walked in?" Glenn exclaimed breathlessly. But he did not wait for Paul to guess, this was too juicy to keep inside. "It's that girl you wanted to meet. The one who played the accordion at the banquet."

Oops, Paul nearly fell looking around through the crowd and not paying attention to the other skaters. Fortunately, Glenn saved him from skating over his own feet.

The music stopped, as did most of the skaters, and Paul and Glenn rolled over to the sidewall while Paul followed Glenn's finger to where Betty and Zada were lacing up their skates.

His heart began to beat faster and faster and he could feel the jitters in his stomach the moment he saw that it really was the beautiful accordion player he had imagined meeting in a thousand ways, under a thousand circumstances.

Just as it had the night at the banquet, those around him faded into the background, the music for the next skate was nonexistent and all he could see and hear through the blur of people was her.

"What do I do?" he finally asked.

"Leave by the back door before she spots you," whispered his jokester cousin being typical Glenn.

"Very funny, Glenn! But now is not the time for joking around! I don't want to mess this up!" Paul said with a serious tone and Glenn knew he was very, very serious.

"Well then," said Glenn, probably a little tongue-in-cheek but Paul did not notice, "That only leaves you one option. Go over and introduce yourself."

Uncharacteristic to his more subdued nature, Paul mustered up the courage to roll over to the bench where Betty and Zada had finished lacing up their skates. There was an uncomfortable moment as he attempted to introduce himself with the words spilling out awkwardly.

"Hello, I'm Pau...um...Paul Nevel...and you play very well...your accord thing..."

Betty could only stare while Zada fought to hold back a snicker. Zada immediately knew what was going on, though her cousin was naïve to it. When a person does not expect love to suddenly appear, they rarely recognize it at first. She forced a grin; what could a woman say to an introduction like that?

"I mean," Paul continued, his mind clearing slightly after the calamitous start, "I saw and heard you at the sports banquet a few weeks ago. You were playing the accordion and I was eating and listening. That is, I had eaten and I was listening. I wasn't eating and listening at the same time..."

He realized how foolish he sounded but he really did not have much experience with this type of thing. He had asked a few girls out in the past but had not had much luck dating. Suddenly he thought perhaps he should run out the back door, as Glenn had previously suggested! But then he figured there was probably no way of recovering from the disaster he had made of it so far, so he went for broke and extended his hand.

"Your name is Betty, if I remember correctly." He knew there was zero percent chance of him not remembering it. He had even kept the program from the banquet just because it had her name on it.

She took his hand; it was not quite a handshake, not quite anything, really. But her hand was soft and wonderful to touch and he did not want to let it go.

"Yes, that's correct. Nice to meet you...Paul."

He liked the way she said his name.

"Betty, may I have the next date…uh I mean skate?" Paul nervously asked.

A little surprised by the bold yet nervous young man, Betty blushed, smiled and said, "Yes, you may."

Well, what else could she do or say? Anyway, he was cute and his shy nature made him endearing. And he still had her hand. Hopefully, he could also skate.

In a continued divine nudge from heaven, the rink announcer called for a slow skate just as Paul, her hand in his, helped her to her feet…or skates. Ye-ow, they were committed.

With her delicate hand in his, they rolled onto the floor to the soft organ music and softer lights. As they found their rhythm skating in step with one another, Paul thought to himself, "Funny how I've been skating in circles for over an hour, but I'm just now feeling dizzy."

They had both slow skated with others before and everyone knew it was common for the guy to take that step of holding a girl's hand because that was just part of couples skating together. Nevertheless, in this age of innocence, it was most often a gesture of respect similar to a man opening the door for a lady. However, both Paul and Betty knew with each lap around the rink that this was different. While Paul had been thinking of Betty for several weeks leading up to their meeting, this was her first introduction to him and the whole thing caught her by surprise. Stunned by the unexpected invitation, she had barely gotten to look at him and tried to steal glances as they glided along and made small talk. A few times his eyes met hers, and his hand felt gentle and strong. They did share one similar sensation; circling the floor, they were oblivious to everyone around them. They were two stars floating in space a million light-years from their nearest neighbor. Then, in what seemed far too quickly, the music stopped and the lights returned to normal. They were both disappointed and excited. There was no need for words; they shared an emotional connection that said it all.

The music picked up tempo. Zada and Glenn joined them for the next skate, faster and one not involving hand-holding, too bad. The four spent the rest of the evening skating together and the men bought the ladies root beer floats in between skates.

Not surprising to Glenn, Paul took him aside before the final skate, "Do you mind if I ask if the girls need a ride?" Paul was the only young guy in his neighborhood with access to a car, so he was always the driver.

Glenn was almost as excited as Paul about the chance to escort two pretty young ladies home. "Do I mind? Are you kidding? This doesn't happen every day you know."

Much too soon, the night's final skate was over and it was time to leave. Paul took a deep breath and asked Betty and Zada together if they wanted a ride home so it did not appear too forward. Nevertheless, no one was fooled about who he really wanted to drive home.

The girls accepted on one condition. They knew they needed permission first. Young ladies did not just accept rides with semi-strange men without first checking with their parents. That meant a wait in the line for the nickel pay phone, but no one seemed to mind. When Betty called her father, he hesitated; he did not recognize the last name.

"Please, Dad. They're good Christian boys, I promise," pleaded Betty.

"Good Christian boy" was the type of phrase that instantly conjured up in the mind of an adult specific qualities in a young man and a perceived code of conduct. A good Christian boy was expected to act in a fashion that would not embarrass his family and church. A good Christian boy had a perceived code of conduct presumed upon him. It meant something and was not used flippantly. Buck conceded.

All four of the young people climbed into Paul's car, a little giddy. The men, as expected, opened the doors for the ladies and made sure their skirts were safely inside before closing them. The conversation was light and Paul took the long way home, of course. Zada's house was first and Glenn politely escorted her to the front door while Paul and Betty waited in the car a bit nervous finding themselves alone. When they arrived at Betty's house, Paul got out of the driver's seat, walked around the car and opened the door for her. Glenn moved from the back to the front seat and waited in the car while Paul walked with Betty along the sidewalk and up the three steps to the front porch.

"I would like you to see me, again." Oooh, even though he had mentally practiced the speech, it still came out so badly.

Regardless, she smiled and said, "Well, I would very much like for me to see you again, too!"

As Paul drove away from Betty's house, he just could not stop smiling. Glenn had never seen his cousin beaming so much. He knew his cousin was falling in love.

When Betty walked into the house, Buck was waiting as fathers did in those days to hear more about this young man who gave her a ride home. "Your mother had a long day and couldn't wait up any longer. She said to tell you goodnight and she wants to hear all about your evening in the morning. So, fill me in!"

Betty tried to suppress the grin on her face but failed. "Oh, he was at the softball banquet a few weeks ago and wanted me to know that he enjoyed listening to me play the accordion. He's very nice and wants to see me again."

"That's it? What else do you know about him?" he inquired.

"Oh, there was this and that," she sighed and filled him in on a few more details.

"Well if you do indeed see him again, I trust he'll come to the door to meet me and your mother. I'll have a written and oral exam ready for him and will judge the results for myself."

Betty looked at her father with concern, but he winked. "And then I'll have to see how he does with a paint brush in his hand."

She giggled, kissed her dad on the cheek and said goodnight. She ran halfway up the stairs, then thought of something and ran back down.

"Oh, and Dad? Thank you so much for going out of your way to drive us to Lakemont." She thought for a moment then spoke mostly to herself, "I had no idea I'd be so glad the Jaffa rink needed those repairs."

She bounced up the stairs, went into her room, took off her shoes, fell back on the bed, closed her eyes and smiled. She thought to herself, "Could this be love at first sight? Be still my heart." She could not wait to tell Marlene, but she was sound asleep. She would tell her in the morning.

The next day the doubts crept into his mind. Paul wondered if Betty really did want to see him again. After all, she was really pretty and could have anyone she wanted. Why would she want to spend time with him? What if she had just been nice to him because she did not want to hurt his feelings?

He decided to take a chance and ask her if he could give her a ride to the skating rink the next week. What if she said no? Well, he would know the truth. He rehearsed and rehearsed then paced and paced in front of the phone. Finally, he made the call.

"Yes," she said and her sweet voice leapt out of the phone and into his ear. "I'd like to ride with you, that would be swell!"

Whew, that had been one of the hardest things he had ever had to do in his young life but he had succeeded.

It seemed like a long week waiting for the weekend to come and when it arrived they had such a great time together. Of course, they had to include Zada and Glenn but they rolled every couple's skate together. It was a new experience for each of them; to actually have a guaranteed partner for each skate was thrilling. They shared knowing looks of quiet pleasure each time a slow skate was called. They even shared a chocolate shake together, two straws, their heads close in an innocent intimate moment.

Skating became a regular shared event. The sign on the Lakemont arena read, "Make a date to roller skate!"

Paul said, "I think it should be 'Bring your date to roller skate!'" He and Betty began to see each other every chance they could. The next several months floated by as fall folded into winter and winter blossomed into spring.

A favorite hangout where they spent many evenings was Taylor's Drive-In, the home of great burgers and fries, delicious milk shakes and ice cream. At Taylor's, patrons could drive up and place their order and carhops brought it right to the car, though not on roller skates as was done some places. Paul usually ordered a chocolate milkshake while Betty would get butter pecan ice cream some days and chocolate chip ice cream on other days. They never seemed to run out of things to talk about. It was a constant source of amusement that they had gone to the same high school and graduated in the same class just the year before, yet had never met. Altoona Area High School was large with over seven hundred students in their class alone. Paul had been in wood shop and other vocational classes that were more geared toward boys, while Betty had taken commercial courses more geared toward girls; consequently, their paths had never crossed. Once when they were comparing reflections on their individual experiences while quietly enjoying the milkshake and ice cream, they both felt compelled at the same time to shout, "Class of 1950, Onward Mid-Centurions!"

For a moment, they stared at each other in surprised astonishment at how closely their minds worked the same, then burst into laughter. They were beginning to understand how they were perfectly made for each other.

Looking out at the blue sky, Betty remembered the day they graduated together yet apart. It was as though she was back there again at the Jaffa Shrine Center with its beautiful Middle Eastern architecture, only this time they were sharing the day as two young lovers venturing out into life as a couple.

In sharing the memories with her, Paul took Betty's hand, a very intimate gesture for the times, and as they looked into each other's eyes, they shouted one more time, "Class of 1950, Onward Mid-Centurions!"

They did not notice those amused and confused expressions around them; they were lost in their budding love.

As the temperatures started to dip and the winter months approached, Paul told Betty he could not wait to go ice skating with her. One Saturday he drove her to Ivyside Park to take a walk. It was a stroll down memory lane for Paul.

As they walked around the lake hand in hand, Paul said, "This is where I learned to ice skate. We've got roller skating down pat and I think we'll make a sensational ice skating couple as well," he said confidently.

"Well, I don't like the bitter cold, but I will look forward to it if I'll be with you." She started to sing, "I really can't stay, baby it's cold outside…"

Not to be outdone, Paul interrupted her singing, "Why do I care how much it may storm? I've got my love to keep me warm."

They laughed as they sat down on a park bench.

He began to reminisce. As a boy, Paul had learned to ice skate at Ivyside Park. It was an amusement park in the 1930s, complete with rides, music, concessions, and picnic grounds. At the time it boasted the world's largest cement swimming pool, where Paul's dad took him and his siblings in the summer to teach them how to swim. It was fed by a spring that came down off of Wopsononick Mountain and was channeled to a shallow warming pond, then passed into the pool. It also made for a large ice skating area in the winter. The park fell on hard times and closed during the Depression, as people did not have money for such extras or even gas to get there. In 1947 the park was purchased by Penn State University. They needed to expand to handle the influx of World War II veterans returning and registering for classes. The main campus being 45 minutes away, this location became the

Altoona branch campus of Penn State. The large bathhouse was turned into space for classrooms, giving it the nickname of "Bathhouse U."

"Did you ever think of going to college, Paul?" Betty asked.

"Well, sure, I've thought about going to something like a trade school, but my family doesn't have the money and besides, I think I can make a career without it. I just want to do right by you…uh…" He blushed and hesitated, "…by whoever…is it whomever? I marry, and be able to support a family. How about you, Betty? Do you want to go to college? I would never want to keep you from something like that."

"I've thought about college, too, but I don't know what I'd study, and it's so expensive. I was fortunate to have good teachers and got good training in the commercial classes at school. I can type pretty fast…"

"Pretty fast?" Paul exclaimed. "I heard you were the fastest in your class, fingers going at lightning speed."

"Oh, who told you that? It was Zada, wasn't it? Or Betty Jane or Marlene? I shouldn't have left them alone with you to tell stories!" She blushed and continued. "I liked shorthand, too, and can take dictation pretty quickly. Mom kept on me to do well in those classes and said I'd need it someday, so I'm glad for that. It got me the job I have now, and I think I'll enjoy being a secretary or bookkeeper."

"And, do you want to have a small family or a large family?" he asked. It was assumed in those days that young ladies wanted to get married and have children as a first priority.

"Oh, I think two or three children would do. Being one of two kids, I can't imagine how your mother managed as one of fifteen," she said wide-eyed.

"Well it sure does make for some fun family reunions. C'mon, let's walk and get some exercise," Paul said to cover up the fact that he had gotten all warm and mushy inside at having broached the topic of having a family with Betty.

Christmas rolled around, their first Christmas as a couple, and Paul bought Betty her first pair of ice skates, a practical gift that he hoped would get lots of use for years to come, as long as he was the one skating by her side. Betty often included Marlene when she went roller skating so she would not feel left out. In addition to its Roller Arena, Lakemont Park had a lake for boating in the summer and ice skating in the winter. Sometimes the visitors would build a huge bonfire along the side of the lake and ice skate under the moonlight. Betty and her friends would act out scenes from movies or practice twirls on the ice and pretend they were stars like Gloria Nord, who was a famous performer on both roller and ice skates in the 1940s. They would make up their own routines to the popular tunes of Bing Crosby, Frank Sinatra, and Perry Como.

The Golden Age of Radio was from the 1930s to the 1950s and a common source of entertainment in America was to gather around the radio to listen to not just the latest music, but more often to favorite radio programs. Just about any kind of story was found around the radio dial; detective shows, comedies, history, literature, live drama, adventure, even horror and science fiction. Paul's favorite was *The Adventures of Champion,* with stories about Gene Autry's horse, Champion, and other cowboys such as Tom Mix. He remembered as a boy listening to country programs on Saturday nights with his dad, especially the Grand Ole Opry with guest appearances by Minnie Pearl. She would tell a few jokes, then say, "I have to get back to the wagon now, 'cause these shoes are killing me."

Betty always enjoyed reading a good mystery, so she convinced Paul to listen to her favorites, *The Shadow* and *Dick Tracy.* When gathered with family and friends, it was always fun to listen to comedy shows such as *Abbott and Costello, Fibber McGee and Molly* and *The Red Skelton Show.* It was good, clean fun with lots of laughs for everyone.

They often went on double dates with Glenn and Zada, who remained just friends, and other friends from church. One evening they were at the soda shop discussing favorite tunes. Glenn said, "I'm thinking about trying out for Benny Goodman."

The other three in unison said, "What?!"

"Yeah, I am. Did you know Dinah Shore auditioned for him and didn't make the cut? The other three shook their heads. "No way."

Glenn continued, "That's right. She didn't make it, so she started her own solo career and look how far she's come! She's a star! I thought maybe I could follow in her footsteps." They all chuckled.

Zada said, "Oh Glenn, we wish you well and remember us when…"

Paul countered, "Don't encourage him." And he gave him a friendly jab in the shoulder. "Hey have any of you heard the latest version of 'Some Enchanted Evening?'"

"Which is the latest – Bing's or Frank's?" Zada asked.

Paul answered, "Well listen, it goes like this:" He began to sing sweetly with his baritone voice, "Some enchanted evening, you will meet a stranger; you may see a stranger, across a crowded room, playing the accordion, and somehow you know, you know even then, that somewhere you'll see her again…"

Betty giggled and said, "Oh, it's the Paul Nevel version!"

Glenn jumped in with, "I've got the second verse: 'Some enchanted evening, when you find your true love, when you feel her call you, across the roller rink; then fly to her side and make her your own; or all through your life, you may skate all alone.'"

They laughed and Zada said, "You two are too much. And I just realized we're the last ones in here. We must've run everyone off!"

Betty said, "Oh my, it's closing time and we've overstayed our welcome." They stood up and prepared to leave. As they walked out, Betty said, "I prefer Nat King Cole, myself. I could just listen to him for hours. I can't seem to get his voice out of my mind."

"Why is that Betty?" Glenn asked.

She thought a moment then replied, "Because his songs are unforgettable."

After the groans came the laughter and the four broke into singing "Unforgettable" as they walked to the car.

The 50s were still a time when most people saw at least one film a week and sometimes more. Betty and her sister Marlene enjoyed going to Lyric Theatre on Fourth Street, which was eight blocks from their home. Paul would often take them when the weather was less than conducive for walking. Their favorite big screen stars were James Dean, Rock Hudson, Marilyn Monroe and Sophia Loren and they especially loved it when the picture show was in color. Occasionally Paul and Betty would go to the drive-in to see a movie.

One lovely day in late March when it seemed the last of the snow and ice had bid farewell and hints of spring were in the air, Paul suggested to Betty that they go for a drive to the scenic lookout on top of Wopsononock Mountain, known to the locals as "Wopsy." It is one of the ridges northwest of Altoona that make up the Allegheny Mountain range. He knew the view was breathtaking, no matter the season. He thought it was also a good time to bring up something he had wanted to ask her.

"How about you drive today, Betty?"

"Very funny, Paul. Do you want to risk your life? You know I can't drive," she answered as they were on their way up the mountain in Paul's car.

"Well, I've been thinking, my dear. How would you like to learn to drive?" he cautiously offered.

"On these curvy mountain roads? No thank you!" she retorted.

"No, silly, I wouldn't ask you to start here. But we could go by the park on our way home and there's a big parking lot with a lot of open space. We could start there. Whadaya say?"

"Hmm, well I'd have to say I have thought about it here and there," she contemplated, "but I just never saw much of a need for it. Mom hasn't ever learned to drive and Dad has always taken us wherever we needed to go, not that we ever ventured far from our end of town."

"Would you like to travel someday? See the ocean? See more of this great country of ours?" he asked.

"Why, yes, I do think I'd like to travel, by car, train, or bus, that is. Flying sounds scary to me; I prefer to keep both feet on the ground. I read about such amazing places in the books from the library, and sometimes look at photography books and dream of seeing such sights."

"You see, I'm thinking if we go on a trip together someday, I might need you to help with the driving," he winked. "Besides, I think it would be great for you to learn and I'd be happy to teach you."

Betty relented and over the next few weeks, Paul taught her to drive. She was never sorry, for it opened more doors of opportunity and independence for her in the future. It was another bond between them, a part of their growing love.

Their shared faith was important to the couple, as well as their circle of family and friends. They were both involved in their respective church choirs and sometimes visited each other's church, especially for special programs. Sundays were sacred and a time to rest and slow down life. It was expected that everyone in the community would respect the day. Shops were closed as well as most restaurants. It was a day for families to gather around the dinner table after church for home-cooked meals, afternoon naps and, in the summer months, sitting on the porch. Sunday visits were common occurrences.

They had both taken jobs after high school; Paul drove a delivery truck for Haller's Bread Company and Betty worked as a secretary at the Metropolitan Life Insurance Company. They were together whenever they could be and the time always seemed to fly. When they were apart, the days seemed to drag along as they anticipated the next time they could be together. Their courtship continued to be an exciting and enjoyable time of growth and discovery for them as individuals and as a couple. Paul worked at being a perfect gentleman and he treated Betty the way a lady ought to be treated. He opened doors for her, carried her packages and always tried to compliment her on her appearance. The latter was not difficult since he thought she was the most beautiful woman he had ever met. Betty admired Paul's many fine qualities as he easily earned her respect and encouragement.

Meanwhile, both sets of parents, James and Murry Nevel, and Buck and Betty Myers, approved of their children dating with their resounding blessings.

More and more, Paul and Betty began to talk of their hopes and dreams for the future, and those hopes and dreams seemed to always include one another. Paul knew he wanted to spend the rest of his life with Betty. He dreamed of the day when she would be known as Mrs. Paul Nevel. They had not known each other very long and their experiences with the opposite sex were very limited, but he knew she was the one and only woman for him. He wanted to ask her to marry him, but what if she did not feel the same way he did, or just was not ready yet? Though they talked about anything and everything, and he was beginning to actually believe she loved him, one subject they seemed to always avoid was a timeline. When was long enough for the courtship to turn to engagement, then marriage, and how was he to know? For Paul, a difficult part of the culture in which they lived was that it was the man's role to broach the idea and the woman's role to decide if she wanted to marry the man.

A new kind of anxiety filled the quiet moments when he thought about how he would pop the question. It was worse than calling her that first time. At least then, all she could do was disappoint him; now she could break his heart. The insecurity within him raised its ugly head as he considered every possible reason why the beautiful accordion player and his roller-skating partner might not want to be his wife. A man in love could go absolutely crazy wondering how to convince the perfect woman that she would be better off becoming his bride.

FOUR

It was a dreary spring Monday the week leading up to the Pittsburgh Pirates' opening day and Paul settled in to listen to the Major League Baseball game broadcast on the radio. The hosts were talking about player stats from last season and who would make the Pirates' starting lineup this year. Paul was much more interested in the Pittsburgh Steelers and a fan of football rather than of baseball, but he liked sports in general. Usually he would have been tuned in, however, today all he could think about was how he wanted to spend the rest of his life with Betty. He had finished his route early and knew she would not be home yet. He tried again to listen so he would be ready with all the right information to impress his church softball buddies on their own opening day, but Paul's mind just kept wandering like the Children of Israel drifting in the desert.

"We haven't known each other very long, but I know she is the one and only woman for me. I can't imagine my life without her," Paul had told Glenn during one of his bolder moments of expressing his feelings. But when his friend and cousin challenged him to just ask her, he could not quite do it. This was a big step, a very big step. Marriage was a life commitment that a person did not go into lightly. He wanted to ask her to marry him, but what if she didn't answer the way he hoped? His heart did flip-flops each time he thought about how he would phrase the question and exactly what the right words would be.

Meanwhile, the radio sports broadcaster was talking about the greatest baseball player to ever live, Babe Ruth. "Ya know, Frank, when Babe talked about how to hit a home run, he said, 'I swing big, with everything I've got. I hit big or I miss big. I like to live as big as I can.'" That's all it took, just what Paul needed to hear. Abruptly, he turned off the radio and, before long, was in his car heading to downtown Altoona.

There it was, on the corner, Walter's Jewelry Store. It was time to see what kind of engagement rings they carried and just how much one would cost. He carefully examined each ring in the glass case and when he saw the one he thought was perfect for Betty, he asked if the man behind the counter would take it out of the case so he could see it up close. When he held the ring in his hand, he knew it was exactly what he wanted. In a moment of truth, he gripped the price tag, said a small prayer and turned it over. Whew, he could breathe again; he could afford it. Thank you God! It even came as a set that included the wedding band too. With a lump in his throat, he told the jeweler he would like to put a deposit down on the set and would be back soon to finalize the purchase. The jeweler placed the rings in a beautiful black box, wrote Paul's name on a sales ticket and put the box in a drawer behind the counter for safekeeping.

His shoulders back, he walked to his car, all the time wondering if he had made the right decision. He was smiling as he thought to himself, "I have the ring, I have the perfect woman and now it is time to swing hard. I will either hit big or miss big, but at least I'll have taken my best swing." His heart was pounding faster than ever as he closed the car door and started the engine.

"Okay," he said aloud to himself, "when the opportunity presents itself, I'll pop the question." Then, looking upward, he said, "And I'll need Your help with this one, Lord!"

With the issue decided, he began rehearsing his speech and planning how he would start the conversation. He could not keep his mind on anything else.

A few days later, the weather had cleared and it was a beautiful evening in April. After an evening of roller skating, Paul drove Betty to her house. Before getting out of the car to go around and open her door, he paused. Betty thought he seemed a little quieter and more contemplative than usual and wondered what might be bothering him.

"Paul? Is everything okay?" she asked. "I'm a little worried that something is wrong. You don't seem yourself."

He turned toward her, his hands trembling as he reached for hers. His brown eyes peered into those beautiful blue eyes he had come to love so much.

Truthfully, she was just a bit afraid.

"Do you think we've known each other long enough to get married?" he asked.

Betty breathed a sigh of relief. Nothing was… Gulp, Betty's heart skipped a beat as her concern turned to sudden delight. "What? Are you asking me to marry you? Oh, Paul. I love you so." She wrapped her arms around him.

Okay, that was not exactly how he thought it would come out, but there it was. He pulled back to look her in the eyes again. "So does that mean yes?"

Her reaction confused him as she was almost in tears. Then she cried, "Yes, honey, yes. I think we've known each other long enough. I would be honored to be your wife." Paul would eventually learn that women burst into tears when they were happy as well as sad.

Paul talked to Betty's father that very evening. With Betty by his side, he asked for permission to marry Buck's daughter. Buck and mother Betty were not surprised and as much as they were sad to see their little girl growing up and spreading her wings, they knew they could not have found a better man if they had gone out searching for him themselves. Buck told Paul he and his wife approved of the marriage and would support them any way they could.

Later, on the front porch, Paul held Betty tightly as they sealed their promise to each other with a kiss. It was the first truly romantic kiss they had together but would definitely not be the last.

As Betty ran up the stairs to her room, she felt as if she were walking on clouds, on pillows of fluffy white bits of heaven. She could hardly believe she was actually going to become Mrs. Paul Nevel. Sitting at her desk, she wrote it out on a piece of paper — Mrs. Paul Nevel, Mrs. Betty Nevel, Mr. and Mrs. Paul Nevel. It had a sweet, sweet sound. Her heart and thoughts were racing so fast and she could not wait to start planning her wedding. She was so happy, then she looked at her hand holding the paper. Had Paul thought to get her a ring? Putting on a nightgown, she dropped into bed but sleep was slow to take her away. As she drifted off to sleep, she tried to be positive, "He is always so thoughtful, he will pick out the perfect ring for me, I'm sure." She sighed and slumber began to claim her. "I can't wait," was her last thought.

After leaving Betty's house, Paul was beyond excited. He shouted to the darkness as he drove and proclaimed to the night sky, "I just asked the most beautiful woman in the world to marry me and she said, 'Yes!'"

He hurried home to tell his parents and his brother Jake. They were as pleased as Betty's parents, offering hugs and hearty congratulations! His heart was still pounding and the adrenaline surged through him so he could barely sleep that night. "Mr. and Mrs. Paul Nevel," he whispered in the quiet of his room. "I sure like the way that sounds, Mr. and Mrs. Paul Nevel. I did it!"

The next day, as soon as Paul's shift ended, he headed downtown to the bank then to Walter's Jewelry Store. When he walked in, he went straight to the counter and said with excitement in his voice, "Well, she said 'Yes!' and I'm here to pick up that black box you put in the drawer for me." He paid the remaining balance, opened the box for one more look, smiled a crooked smile, thanked the Jeweler and headed out. He could have flown home but the car had to get back to the house somehow so he decided the sensible thing was to drive it there.

The Saturday before Easter in 1952, Paul planned to spend the afternoon with Betty. Instead of just handing the black box to her, he wanted to do something special. So on his way to her house, he stopped at his Aunt Dot's corner store to buy a few things. When he told his aunt what he was up to, she excitedly got in on the game and helped him choose some items. Then he was off to see his fiancé and make it official with the ring!

When Paul arrived at Betty's house, he was carrying a large shopping bag, which made her curious and, with a twinkle in his eye, he held it out towards her. "For you, my dear."

She looked inside and giggled as she pulled out an adorable Easter basket he had put together just for her, filled with some of her favorite treats. She saw jelly beans, a white chocolate bunny and assorted penny candies.

"There are surprises in the plastic eggs." He pointed out a pastel yellow egg and said, "Open that one."

She shook it a little to see if she could guess what was inside. "Sounds like more jelly beans." She opened it to find cashew nuts, her favorite. Paul had a bowl and she dumped the contents into it. She was enjoying the game and tickled by his unusually playful manner. This was a new side of Paul and she was pleased to see it. After a couple of eggs, the game became guessing what type of treat might be in each of them. She opened others and found more assorted candies and nuts that were added to the bowl.

"Are you trying to fatten me up?" She joked.

Then Paul motioned to the last egg, "Let's see, why don't you open the pink one now? Any guesses?"

She shook it but it did not make a sound. "Hum, I don't know what this could be."

As she pulled it apart, she found tissue inside.

"A tissue?" Betty had no idea why her man would give her a tissue. Then she felt something inside.

She glanced up at Paul and he was grinning from ear to ear. She carefully unwrapped the tissue and, there it was, a sparkling diamond set in a shiny gold ring. She gasped and could not believe her eyes, now brimming with tears. A ring!! It was so beautiful, the most beautiful ring she had ever seen.

This time, Paul understood that tears were good, they were great tears.

The tissue served a second purpose as she used it to wipe the moisture from her eyes.

"Are you still sure about marrying me?" he asked. "This is your chance to back out."

At first, she could not speak. Of all the things to find in a pink plastic Easter egg, an engagement ring was the last she expected.

She managed to answer through the stream flowing down her cheeks, "More than ever!" The romantic moment was more real and more special than anything Hollywood could put in any film shown at the Lyric Theatre on Fourth Street.

He gently took the ring from her shaking hand and slipped it onto her finger. It was a perfect fit, just as they were a perfect fit for each other. Once again, Paul sealed his love with a kiss.

Holding out her hand with the ring, Betty could not believe what a loving, sensitive fella she was about to marry. Surely she was blessed by God.

Easter Sunday was glorious, indeed. Betty had to be at the church early to warm up with the choir and for them to don their choir robes. Her friends gathered around as she told them how Paul surprised her with the Easter basket and how excited he was when she opened the pink egg. Then she held out the ring for them to see as they ooh-ed and ah-ed. She never tired of telling the story and her friends loved hearing all about it. Paul was in his own church's choir for a special Easter cantata, so they could not attend church together that day. He told Glenn first, then the other guys about the proposal. He received hearty slaps on the back and attaboys. As the news trickled out around the church that day, he heard lots of congratulations and there were interesting looks from some of the ladies. After the service, Paul was giving Glenn a ride home when he asked if he minded if they picked up Betty from her church on the way. When they pulled up to the curb near the door, she came outside and asked the men if they would come in for a few minutes. Some people wanted to see the man who proposed with an Easter basket! The happy newly-engaged couple was the talk of Easter Sunday; that is, second to Jesus rising from the dead, of course! Once again Paul had to deal with the strange, adoring looks the ladies of the church gave him; they thought he was so romantic.

And Glenn, well Glenn was Glenn, in that characteristically humorous way he had. He leaned over Paul as they watched the giggling women gathered around Betty, tongue in cheek, and said, "John Wayne would not have proposed using an Easter basket and a pink egg."

But Paul took the good-natured ribbing in stride, "John Wayne isn't marrying the prettiest girl in Altoona."

"Good point," frowned Glenn. "Come to think of it, neither am I." He feigned disappointment then the two men laughed as yet another young lady joined the circle, had to see the ring and insisted that Betty tell the story all over again. Paul could only force an embarrassed smile as the ladies glanced over in admiration, and with a few envious snickers.

The date was set. The wedding would take place on Friday, August 29, 1952 at Second Avenue Evangelical United Brethren Church, as traditionally a wedding would be held at the bride's home church. They asked the Reverend Max Houser from Betty's church to officiate. He said he would be honored to be a part of Paul and Betty's wedding.

There was so much to be done to get ready for the big day. The next few months found Paul and Betty both working hard and saving as much money as they could. Betty, Marlene and their mother were busy with the details. Meanwhile, whenever possible Paul and Betty were trying to spend their free time together. Paul had no idea there were so many things to consider when planning a wedding.

Betty wanted her sister Marlene to be her maid of honor, which meant Paul would need to ask someone to be his best man. "Betty, what do think about Glenn as the best man?" She agreed that Glenn was the perfect choice. Glenn was thrilled when Paul asked him to be the best man. After all, he liked to remind Paul, he was the one that got things rolling that night at the roller rink. So of course, his spot in the wedding party was well deserved!

Betty's dream was to wear a simple yet elegant white gown and veil on her wedding day. She, her mom and Marlene found the perfect dress at Lucretia's Bridal Shop in downtown Altoona. They also found dresses for the bridesmaids that matched Betty's white dress, only in pink, yellow and blue. Betty was so excited and could not wait to tell Paul all about it.

Sitting on the Myers' front porch swing, they caught up with each other about the day. She was chattering away about how the arrangements were working out so well and how great this was and that was. Then she noticed that she seemed to be the only one with any enthusiasm. She expected him to be excited too, but instead he looked confused.

"Paul, is everything okay?" she asked tentatively. "I thought you would be glad to know that we found all the dresses today."

"Um," that is how men start conversations when they do not know how to start conversations. "Um." There was always that long silence as they sought the words. "Well, Betty, I didn't know you were adding two bridesmaids to the wedding. I thought it was just going to be you and me, Marlene and Glenn."

There was a long pause.

"Well it can't be just you and Glenn or the wedding party will be unbalanced."

"Um." He thought for a second. "The wedding party needs to be balanced? Who made that rule?"

"It's not a rule." Betty was stunned by Paul's unexpected lack of understanding. With tears welling up in Betty's eyes, she said, "Zada is not only my cousin, but one of my closest friends. She was with me the first time I met you! And Betty Jane and I, being neighbors, have always talked about how we would be in each other's weddings when we grew up."

"Um," he said, then stopped for a very long minute. Finally, he continued, "I don't exactly know how to choose two other guys to have up there with me."

The tears were no longer contained and slid down her cheeks.

Oh, tears, Paul knew instinctively that these were not happy tears. He had said something very wrong, very bad.

"You have plenty of friends," she snapped back, then blew her nose and wiped her eyes.

"Why does this have to be so complicated?" he blurted out.

"It's not that complicated," she replied angrily now, "You have three friends with you and I have three friends with me. How hard is that to understand?"

He was taken aback. He had not expected such a response. He had never considered that he would have to have someone other than Glenn. He had no idea who to ask, how to ask them or if they would even agree. He was about to express his own frustration when he opened his mouth and very strange words came out, "Um, do they have to wear pink, yellow and blue suits?"

Abruptly, Betty stopped crying and looked up at her fiancé. She could tell from his facial expression that he was serious. She laughed and he laughed just because she was laughing. Then they laughed together.

"No, they do not have to wear pink, yellow and blue suits," she reassured him. "In fact, I would prefer that they didn't."

The tension was broken.

"So now I need to choose two more men to be in the wedding? I don't know who else to ask," mused Paul. "Who would they be…?"

What could have been their first real fight became a learning experience. In his male mind, a friendship had to be very close to invite another man to be part of such a special occasion. His brother Jake would have been his first choice, but he knew Jake did not own a suit and he would not put his brother in an awkward position of feeling like he had to come up with the money to rent one. He would have gladly bought Jake a suit himself, if he had the means to do so. She had unwittingly placed him in a position where he was not comfortable.

They both sat quietly, staring down. "I'm sure we can work this out," she whispered. "That's what marriage is all about."

Paul put his arms around her and said, "Betty, honey, I'm sorry. I love you so much and I guess I let all these wedding plans get to me. I can't wait for you to be my wife."

He thought for a moment, "Since I can't ask Jake," he sighed, "I'll ask my good friend, Kenny and Glenn's brother, George."

She looked at her man and saw the pride in his face; he had met the problem head-on and solved it. "Paul, I love you too and I'm sorry too."

Paul wiped the tears from Betty's cheeks and said, "Want to go get some ice cream?"

She smiled in return and said, "Yes! I would love to! How about some chocolate chip ice cream at Taylor's Drive-In?"

The trip to the restaurant was a celebration of overcoming a major obstacle together, though neither expressed it in that way.

Paul ordered his usual, a chocolate milk shake and Betty enjoyed a delicious cup of chocolate chip ice cream. There was nothing like very best friends sharing ice cream.

"I'm so glad Uncle Paul gave me that suit last year when I graduated," Paul said after an enjoyable long pull on his straw. Shakes were always a challenge getting the first glob up the straw when fresh and thick. "Did I ever tell you about that?"

"No, but I'd love to hear about it," Betty replied.

He savored a slurp of milkshake as he remembered, "Yeah, he bought me my first and only suit as a high school graduation gift. He said to me, 'I can't let my namesake receive his diploma in his farmer overalls.' Then, with a big smile, he gave me a gray Gabardine suit."

Buoyed by the remembrance, he leaned over and kissed Betty and said, "I wore the suit at graduation, which you apparently did not see, and now I'll wear it on the best day of my life. The day you become Mrs. Paul Nevel. Hopefully, you'll see it then."

Betty blushed and kissed Paul on the cheek, leaving a little smear of chocolate chip ice cream he had to wipe off with a napkin. Yep, she was enjoying her favorite treat with her favorite guy. Life could not get any better.

The next day, as soon as Paul finished with his deliveries for Haller's Bread Company, he stopped by Kenny's house and asked him if he would stand by him at the wedding. Kenny said, "Betty must be quite the catch. I've never seen you so happy. I would be glad to do that for you, my friend." Paul and Kenny spent some time talking about baseball and some of the great players that were coming along; Mickey Mantle, Hank Bauer and Yogi Berra. Kenny boasted that the Yankees, his favorite team, were expected to dominate professional baseball. Paul said, "Don't be too sure this far out; pride comes before a fall, ya know? I'm still hoping the Pirates will have a good year."

So, pondered Paul, this balanced wedding was paying off with a renewed friendship. Who would have thought?

Since Paul had one more stop to make, he had to keep moving. "Great catching up with you, Kenny. See you at the wedding rehearsal."

"Thanks for asking me, it means a lot," replied Kenny.

Then Paul headed over to see George next. When his cousin came outside, they talked about music and sports for a few minutes and then Paul told George why he was there. He asked him to be a groomsman and, just like his brother, Glenn and friend Kenny, George said he would be happy to take part in the wedding. He told Paul he knew Betty had to be special because he had never seen his cousin floating so far off the ground.

"Thanks, George. You got a suit to wear?"

"Is that why you asked me to be in your wedding?" he said with a chuckle as he patted Paul on the back.

"No, I just wanted to make sure you weren't going to show up in your overalls."

They both laughed and Paul headed to his car. As he pulled out of the driveway, he waved at George and yelled, "Thanks, Cuz. See you at the wedding rehearsal."

He began to think maybe weddings were good for bringing people together but he was happy to only do it once in his life. It was a lot of work. He went through the list of things left to do before the wedding as he drove. "Almost done," he thought. "Oh, what about the honeymoon?"

After some consideration, he decided to ask Betty. It did seem to be a decision a couple would make together. Anyway, he wanted to make it a very special time for both of them.

As word got around, there were plenty of congratulations and excitement among their family and friends. A longtime member of First Church of Christ, Mrs. Pope approached Paul after choir practice one evening. They had her on their list to ask her to sing during the ceremony.

"I heard the good news, Paul. Congratulations. Betty seems to be such a lovely person," she said.

Paul was gratified. The consensus of the community was that he could not have made a better choice for a wife. He wondered what was being said about him, but Glenn told him not to worry. What he heard was all good.

Anyway, Paul replied, "Thank you very much! I feel like I don't deserve her, but she said yes so I hope she knows what she's getting herself into!"

"Well if she is half as special as you are Paul, I'm sure you deserve each other and the good Lord has brought you together."

"We certainly believe He has! And while I'm speaking with you, we wanted to ask you something. We would be very honored if you would be the soloist at our wedding. Will you please consider it, Mrs. Pope?"

"Oh my, of course, I would love to! The honor is all mine. Just let me know what songs you choose."

"I imagine Betty already has some songs in mind, though she hasn't clued me in yet! I already asked Mr. Franz if he would play the organ, and he said he'd be happy to. The wedding will be at Betty's church, and I'm sure they'll be glad to oblige with rehearsal time."

"That sounds wonderful. I always enjoy having Roy accompany me and we're used to working together. Don't you worry any more about it. You'll have enough on your plate. We'll take care of the music end of things."

"Thank you so much, Mrs. Pope. It means so much to me, to us."

FIVE

Second Avenue Evangelical United Brethren Church was filled with the Nevel and Myers families and friends from all over the area. As Roy Frantz played the wedding march on the organ, Buck appeared with his beautiful daughter prepared to walk down the aisle to an appreciative Paul in his gray Gabardine suit, almost too captivated by his bride to remember what to do next.

Fortunately, this was not Reverend Houser's first wedding and he knew exactly how to deal with fumbling grooms and blushing brides. As well, Paul had Glenn beside him with Kenny and George smartly attired in their suits, none of them pink, yellow or blue, and ready to catch him if he fell or trap him if he tried to run. That was all discussed by the men in the pastor's office before the ceremony, with Glenn taking charge of the emergency contingency plans. To relieve his cousin's nervousness, he even made a joke about losing the ring. Now, that did not go over as well as Glenn might have liked but the expression of relief on Paul's face when he showed the groom the ring was priceless.

When the bride entered at the back of the sanctuary, she thought that she had the most handsome groom any girl could want waiting for her at the altar. Preceding her down the aisle was Zada in her yellow bridesmaid dress and Betty Jane in blue, then her lovely sister Marlene as maid of honor in pink.

When it was time for the bridal march, Betty's mother stood up on cue, which in turn cued the audience to stand. She felt faint for a moment, then thought, "If my daughter can keep from fainting, then I had better as well." She turned and watched as her handsome husband, looking dapper in his suit, proudly escorted their first-born down the aisle. His eyes were moist as he gave her away, lifting her veil to kiss her on the cheek, and joining his wife in the first pew. The minister gave permission for the audience to be seated. Betty leaned over and whispered to Buck, "Well done, dear. It's been awhile since I've seen you dressed in anything but your painting clothes. You clean up pretty well!" She took his hand and looked at their fingers laced together. "Oh Buck, look at that paint under your nails!" He knew she was just trying to avoid the emotion of the moment. "Hush, we have a wedding to watch. I'll let you clean my nails later." She elbowed him and proceeded to try to behave herself.

The couple repeated their vows and listened to Mrs. Pope sing her rendition of "The Lord's Prayer." But, truth be told, they were so caught up in each other that they barely remembered the details. Paul had to wake himself up from the dream when he heard, "You may kiss the bride." It was their first very public kiss, a little awkward and short but sweet. The next thing they knew, Reverend Houser was introducing them as Mr. and Mrs. Paul Nevel, and they were walking past their friends and family to the back of the church.

Cake, ice cream and other refreshments were served at the reception, which took place in the church social hall, the very same room where Paul first laid eyes on Betty just days shy of a year prior. The wedding party stood in a line, along with both Paul's and Betty's parents, as the guests came through and congratulated the new couple. None were more pleased than Uncle Paul who considered the cost of the suit as money well spent since it served two memorable occasions. While cutting the cake and eating the ceremonial first bite, Paul did not quite manage to hit Betty's mouth and smeared a small dab of frosting on her nose. To the cheers of those assembled, she got Paul back with a glob of frosting on his.

Refreshments consumed, gifts opened and congratulations expressed, it was time for the great getaway. The announcement was made that the bride and groom were about to make their exit and the guests made their way outside for the send-off. Kenny and George were in charge of passing out the rice and making sure everyone had a healthy handful. The kids especially relished the opportunity to participate. The fleeing couple was showered in white as they made for their car in a tradition dating back to ancient times that became popular in the United States. To throw rice on the newlyweds as they left symbolized the showering of abundance on the couple, wishes for fertility and a fruitful, wealthy and prosperous union. The grain signified the fact that a small seed can grow into a large crop. Though it is doubtful that any of those throwing rice that day gave much deep thought to the meaning behind the tradition, their well wishes would come true as it would prove to be prophetic in ways they would not have dreamed.

When discussing where to go for their honeymoon, Paul and Betty both knew they could not afford to spend much because money was tight and they had to spend most of what they had saved on the wedding expenses and getting their own apartment. In the early 50s, hotels were neither plentiful nor inexpensive and they definitely could not afford to travel to a resort area. However, Glenn offered a suggestion. With the Labor Day holiday on Monday, many of the couple's church friends would be spending the last weekend of the summer at the annual young adult retreat at Camp Christian in southwestern Pennsylvania. This was the church camp Paul and Glenn had attended with their youth groups for retreats and weeks of camp throughout their school years. Paul was excited to take Betty to see the camp sometime, as it held wonderful memories for him, but it was not exactly what he had in mind for a honeymoon. Unfortunately, they had few options to make the honeymoon weekend special, so Paul presented the idea to Betty. Ooh, she was not so sure that was a good idea. Well, for obvious reasons but they were not the kind of reasons polite people discussed in public conversations. Though she was hesitant, she agreed when Paul told her that Glenn was working out a deal with the camp manager to secure a private cabin for the couple. And he made her a promise; when they were able to afford it, he would take her on a real honeymoon, regardless of how long that took. So, a honeymoon at church camp it would be. However, they were glad they would have their first night alone in the apartment where they would make their first home together.

The first night together was not one many couples of the era of the 50s discussed or planned. Consequently, they were in the unchartered territory of love's great mystery. All of their lives, they were taught that the greatest gift two young people in love could give to each other was their fidelity. They were stepping into the unknown together on an adventure of discovery. The heavens smiled as this husband and wife whom God had brought together became one, not unlike the type of relationship that God desires to have with His people; intimate, caring and filled with love.

The next morning as the sun rose higher in the sky and brightened the bedroom, Paul woke with a start. What time was it? Was he late for work? Then he felt Betty beside him and relief washed over him as he remembered pleasantly. He put his arm around her as she stirred.

"Good morning, my love. I thought for a moment I was dreaming, but this is for real, isn't it? Here you are with me. We are married!" He tried to let it sink in a little. "What were we thinking when we said we'd go to camp today?"

Betty turned toward him and put her hand to his cheek, feeling his morning stubble, and said she felt the same way. It was like a dream, but she was awake. "Do we have to go, honey? Can't we just stay here and hide away together for the weekend?"

"I suppose we could call in sick!" Paul raised his eyebrows and smiled. "But, they're expecting us and we wouldn't want to disappoint. It'll be fun and I'll make sure we get some time to ourselves. I just hope Glenn and the boys don't come serenading us in the middle of the night!"

"I wouldn't put it past them. I've heard the stories about the midnight crooning and serenades between the boys' and girls' cabins," Betty said. "I do admit I'm looking forward to meeting more of your friends and hearing more stories!"

"I heard the speaker for the weekend is really good, and you'll enjoy the hymn sings. Let's take your accordion. Hey and I'll finally have a girl who will sit with me at campfire. You will be my date, won't you?"

"You've got that right and I'm not letting you out of my sight."

Paul pulled her close and looked into her eyes. "And I'm not letting you out of mine."

A few hours later, they set out for camp. After the nearly three-hour drive, they arrived to a large spray-painted sign on cardboard at the camp entrance reading, "Welcome Newlyweds, Mr. & Mrs. Paul Nevel! Congratulations!" When they drove closer to the circle of cabins, they could not miss which one was theirs. "Honeymoon Suite" was in big, colorful letters on a sign hung on the door. When the others saw them drive up, they ran to the couple, whooping and hollering with great fanfare. Someone even had a camera and wanted them to pose for pictures.

"So much for being discreet and kind of just sliding in here as two of the campers," Paul said a little red-faced from blushing.

They participated in afternoon recreational events, told stories of camp memories around the table during the evening meal with the other young adult campers and then it was time for the hymn sing in the chapel. Glenn talked Betty into getting out her accordion; after all, she did not bring it along to let it sit in the car, did she? The speaker shared an encouraging message of God's love and His plan and purpose for each life. He talked about how living out that purpose by trusting and depending on God would affect positive change in the world. He could not pass up an opportunity to use the newlyweds as an example. Their story demonstrated his very point.

"Take this couple for instance, married for only about twenty-four hours." There was applause. He continued, "I heard a little of their story earlier, how they met and fell in love. Do you think it was by accident, Paul, that you saw this lovely young lady playing her instrument and wanted to meet her, prayed about it and a few weeks later ran into her at the skating rink?"

Paul said emphatically, "No sir!"

"And how about you, Betty," the preacher continued. "Do you think it was by chance that the first skating rink you went to was closed that night, and you ended up at the same one where Paul was, after he had desperately prayed that God would allow him to see you again?"

Before she could answer, Glenn piped up, "I spotted her first! He might've missed her in the crowd if it wasn't for me!"

Everyone laughed.

The preacher said, "Glenn, the Lord knows and now we all know you were part of the plan."

More laughter followed.

"Uh, where were we…Betty?"

She shook her head. "No, I don't believe it was by chance. So much has happened that was clearly orchestrated by Someone bigger than us."

He went on to encourage the couple. "Well, I say God brought you together because He had a plan. He knew you'd make a better team together than you would as individuals apart. What better way to start a marriage than to be out here in God's country with God's people, asking God's blessing on your lives and marriage? He has a plan for you and your life together. If you trust Him, He'll bless you, your children, your grandchildren, and even their children! Same with the rest of you here, same with me. It comes down to trusting that God is who He says He is. God is love. We all leave a legacy, every one of us, good or bad. What kind of legacy do you want to leave? It's up to you."

He concluded with a prayer of blessing.

They sang one last song and filed out of the chapel. The mood was reflective, upbeat and someone suggested, "It's still light enough out, let's go up to Vesper Rock."

The place was an outdoor chapel of sorts, with several rows of stone benches and a large pulpit made of stone, with a cross etched into the front of it. They started walking into the woods and one of the men started singing, "We are climbing Jacob's ladder…" The others joined in, singing the old spiritual while they climbed the steep path leading up the hill.

Paul took Betty's hand. "This is one of the places I wanted to show you. God really spoke to my heart up here a few times. I like being outside to pray, where I can see His creation all around."

The group sang and hiked and soon reached Vesper Rock. Some sat on the benches while others took turns standing in the pulpit just for fun and looking out at the view. It was getting dark, so they walked back down the path to the Millhouse to enjoy the evening snack, ice cream sundaes. Then it was time for Paul to walk his date to the campfire under the stars and a time of singing.

After a few lively songs, on the third verse of "Kum Ba Yah," it seemed the opportune time for the couple to sneak away to their honeymoon suite. Paul took Betty by the hand and they stealthily vanished, or at least as surreptitiously as was possible for newlyweds that were immediately missed when it was noticed that they were gone.

The cabin was small, one room with four bunk beds. The camp manager had pushed a couple of the bunks together to make a double bed and brought nice bedding from his own house to accommodate them, leaving flowers in a vase on a dresser under a mirror. It was rustic, but quaint, and it had a lock on the door for which they were thankful, especially knowing Glenn and the guys might be roaming and up to their midnight antics. The bathhouse was a short walk away; the men's section on one end of the building and ladies' on the other side, complete with toilets, sinks, showers, usually some type of creepy crawlies and often a frog or two.

When they both returned from the bathhouses to the cabin, Paul embraced Betty as he said, "What a day, huh? Was our wedding really just last night? Betty, I apologize; it's not the Hilton, and you, my wife, certainly deserve the Hilton. But at least it's our own little space. I hope you'll be comfortable enough to sleep, Sweetheart. That is, if I let you sleep!" He winked and kissed her.

"It's been a wonderful day, Paul. I've really enjoyed it. So much love and encouragement here. Can you believe how the preacher pointed us out? It's a lot to think about. And what a beautiful setting, out away from the cities and here in these mountains. I've never been much of a country girl, but I suppose I could learn to be one. God has been good to us and we have lots to be thankful for. Who am I to complain? Besides, I'm with you and that's all that matters. That is, as long as one of those frogs I saw in the bathroom didn't follow us in here!"

Lying together in the makeshift double bed with the top bunks overhead, the soft noises of the other campers outside, love carried them away into the night.

SIX

The young couple settled into their small second floor apartment at 1204 6th Avenue. It was ideally located where Paul only had a few blocks to walk to work at Haller's Bread Company. Betty had to go a little farther with her daily walk to the Metropolitan Life Insurance Company which took her over the 12th Street walking bridge.

Betty had learned to cook from her mother and was not shy about trying new recipes that she thought Paul would like. When they both had long work days, she would tell him to rest while she prepared, but he all too often offered to help by stirring the pot or setting the table.

"I'm a meat and potatoes man, ya know, not too hard to please," he would remind her when she lamented about the lack of time to prepare something special.

"You mean a meat-and-potatoes-and-something-chocolate-for-dessert man, right?" she responded teasingly and started singing, "If I knew you were coming, I'd have baked a cake..."

"Well, Mrs. Nevel, you know me better than I thought," he said as he twirled her around and tenderly kissed her. "And you know I'll take a kiss from you over chocolate anytime."

Settling into his arms, she replied, "Oh good, because we're out of cocoa and a kiss will have to do tonight."

So he kissed her again. They were really enjoying this miracle called marriage and their life together.

Altoona, Pennsylvania was founded in 1849 by the Pennsylvania Railroad as a site for a workshop and maintenance complex. The railroad tracks divided the town, as they did many towns and cities when railroads expanded in the mid-1800s, becoming the main transporter of goods and people.

The bridge which Betty crossed on her way to work went over the tracks.

"Someday," she often thought as she gazed down at a passing train or at the tracks disappearing into the distance, "I am going to take a ride on one of those trains, one that goes around the Horseshoe Curve so I can see it from the train for myself."

The Pennsylvania Railroad's 2375-foot long Horseshoe Curve was considered to be one of the most incredible engineering feats in the world. It was built to navigate through the Allegheny Mountains just outside of Altoona and complete the railway system across the state. Constructed mostly by hand and without heavy equipment, hundreds of Irish immigrants worked twelve-hour days for a mere twenty-five cents per hour. It took over three years to complete but when it opened in 1854, travel time by rail from Philadelphia to Pittsburgh was reduced from several days to just thirteen hours.

One evening after dinner, Paul was reading the newspaper and Betty was glancing through a book about Pennsylvania history.

"Paul, have you seen the Horseshoe Curve?"

"Sure, who hasn't?"

She stared at him for a moment to gauge if he was making fun of her. He appeared serious so she said, "Well, I haven't…at least not that I remember. I think we went there when I very young. I've read about it and of course learned about it in school and think it's fascinating. When I was about 10 years old, dad was going to take us up there to the park where you can watch the trains come and go. Marlene and I were so excited. But before the weekend came, it was all over the news that it had been closed, something to do with it being a target site for the Nazis."

"Yeah, I remember people talking about it. It's strange to think that Hitler actually knew about our city."

In fact, the Horseshoe Curve was on the list carried by four Nazi infiltrators the Coast Guard captured off the coast of Long Island, New York. The German spies had twelve places important to U.S. industry which they planned to sabotage. Through a comedy of errors, the Nazi mission fell apart and the men were caught along with four other German agents. All eight were tried as spies, two received long prison sentences and the other six were executed.

"Thank goodness, honey. Can you imagine Nazis infiltrating our town to blow up the railroad?" She shuddered at the thought. "I remember that we waited for it to reopen, but it was kept closed for several years. Will you take me there sometime?"

Paul lowered his paper, "Are you asking me out on a date?"

With a twinkle in her eye, Betty answered, "Well, we do have an anniversary coming up on Friday…"

Paul looked at her, confused. Anniversary…? Marriage was full of surprises and one thing he was learning was that women marked special times and places.

"Two months on Friday," she continued playfully. "I think it would be the perfect opportunity for you to whisk me away for a day."

"Great idea. The leaves will be pretty, too. Let's plan to do it on Saturday; we'll make a day of it." Paul grinned.

Betty clapped her hands together with excitement. "I'll finally get to see the Horseshoe Curve and better yet with the man of my dreams - on a Saturday."

"The date is on then. I'll pick you up at 9 a.m.," Paul winked.

Betty stood, her hands on her hips. "You think you can pick me up?"

"I believe that I can." With that, Paul tossed his paper aside, stood and swept her off her feet.

They were young and full of energy and passion. For Paul, every day was a celebration.

As the newlyweds settled in, Betty worked to keep the apartment tidy and clean, free of dust and clutter. Paul appreciated returning home to a neat house, though it did not come as naturally for him to pick up after himself and put things in their place. She had to train him to rinse his whiskers out of the sink after he shaved and put the toilet seat down.

"I pity Myra Sue, having to grow up with you boys and your messes," she teased him.

Sometimes it felt like nagging to him, but that all washed away when he considered that he had it pretty darn good.

To Betty, it was all part of her share of the partnership they had formed, which was how she explained her feelings to Marlene while roller skating.

"I have to say, Sis, even though we did our share of complaining about cleaning up our rooms, I'm glad Mom is a good housekeeper and it rubbed off on me," Betty acknowledged. "As for Paul, well, he'd rather just drop his clothes and let them lie. I don't know how he thinks they magically disappear then reappear in his dresser drawers, clean and smelling good."

Marlene just giggled and said, "But he's so dreamy, big sister..." Then she stopped and blushed realizing what she had said about her sister's husband. "I mean handsome and kind hearted. That has to make up for some of it."

And it did, which was why Betty smiled. "Of course. I love him more every day. Just didn't know how dirty a man's socks could get. Just warning you for when it's your turn."

She winked and released Marlene's hand as they took another turn.

"I'll race you." Betty chided her sister then pushed off on her roller skates to rush ahead.

"No fair, you got a head start," Marlene called after her.

Marlene had taken a job at Metropolitan when she graduated high school and Betty appreciated having her "little" sister at the office with her. When Paul was working late, she would ride home with Marlene and have dinner with her and their parents.

Because Paul worked odd jobs in the evenings or on weekends, Betty socialized with her sister and old high school friends when he was busy. Still, she always missed Paul when it came to the slow skate and having a milkshake all to herself just was not as much fun as sharing it.

One evening, Glenn went with Paul so that he could introduce him to one of his customers in need of some work done. Glenn was a salesman for Allegheny Electronics and a customer expressed the need for someone to make a few minor repairs around the house. Always ready to support his cousin, Glenn gave out Paul's number. Glenn rode with Paul when he went to see what was required and to give the estimate. On the drive over to the job site the two had some lighthearted conversation about how marriage was treating Paul. He asked Glenn how things were going with his latest flame. He reveled in turning the marital tables on his friend by kidding him about his status as a single man and the prospects for getting married. Unexpectedly though, the conversation took a turn and became very serious. Glenn's thoughts were not on romance but bigger issues.

"Did you see the news?" was all that Glenn had to say.

Indeed, Paul had. He read about it every day and listened to the radio news when Betty was not in the room. The Korean War had begun to cause havoc among many average American families. National Guard units were being called up and sent over to the conflict and casualties were mounting. President Truman had earlier decided not to seek formal authorization from Congress, and it came back to haunt him when the hostilities became stalemated. Dubbed "Mr. Truman's War" by legislators, particularly in the opposition, the President seemed determined to expand the war.

The two young men voiced their mutual concerns about how international events might affect them. They shared the same views on the politics of the situation, as well as the same fears of what the future might hold for them. They were loyal American citizens. However, there was a certain uncertainty in planning their lives when those plans could easily be interrupted. And they were.

One cold November evening, the doorbell for the Nevels' apartment rang. There seemed an urgency to the doorbell's ringing, if that were even possible, so Paul ran down the stairs and opened the door to find Glenn on the other side.

"Hey Glenn, get yourself in here before you freeze to death," Paul said.

Instantly though, he saw by Glenn's face that something was wrong, very wrong. His cousin carried with him an official-looking envelope which he showed to Paul.

Paul said quietly, "Come on upstairs. Betty is folding laundry in the bedroom."

Cautiously, Glenn glanced into the other room while he showed his cousin the white paper letter. Across the top it read, "Selective Service System – Order to Report for Induction."

"I'm being drafted," he whispered.

Regrettably, that was the moment Betty entered. From the expressions on the two men's faces, she knew something was not right. "What is it fellas? What is the matter?"

Regardless of the fact that Glenn had whispered, she still heard him, but she did not want to believe what she thought she heard. She also paid attention to the news reports though she did not discuss her fears and knew women at the insurance company whose men had been called into the military. The new bride was very aware that her husband might be next and she prayed many a night since their engagement and wedding that it would not happen.

"It's a draft letter, Betty," replied Paul. "Did you happen to bring in the mail today?"

Betty barely got out, "No, I didn't," when Paul bolted back down the stairs to check the black metal mailbox on the porch by the door. Among some advertisement fliers, there was an envelope exactly like the one Glenn had. His stomach churning, he looked out from the porch to the starry sky and asked God for strength before he hurried back upstairs to open the envelope.

"Oh no, oh no, this can't be," Betty shook her head while she and a glum Glenn waited. "What does this mean?"

A sober Paul returned with the day's mail and the envelope. His hands shaking, he ripped it open with Betty and Glenn looking over his shoulders. It contained the same message. The men compared letters and saw that both were required to report to the same local induction station on the same day.

"No, no, no," Betty could not believe the news. "You're married. They can't send a married man with a new wife away!"

"Yes they can," responded Paul. "They can and they will."

As was the case with most Americans of that era, they were patriots and they shared a sense of duty to their country. Their opinion of the war was irrelevant. Their country called them into service and they would go.

They shared a few tears and hugs and, as was his way, Glenn offered a light-hearted salute then left to visit his parents and break the troubling news to them.

It was a quiet evening as Paul and Betty sat very close to one another on the sofa and talked softly, each trying to make the other feel better.

"We'll get through this. I'll be back soon," stated Paul definitively. "Promise me you'll wait for me. We will have a bright future together when all of this is over. I love you forever."

"Forever is a long time," whispered Betty, her head on his shoulder and her eyes filled with tears. "Soon is not fast enough."

It was a sleepless night for the couple. In a scene happening all over the country, the draft had come and war was about to interrupt their peaceful world.

SEVEN

Paul and Glenn arrived as instructed at the induction center. They were two healthy young men, therefore there was no reason to not accept them into the military.

It was a mere month later that they were on their way to their Army posts. Paul and Betty had decided that it would be best for Betty to move back in with her parents so she would not be alone and they could save money; the apartment seemed more a luxury than a necessity. Packing their clothes and few possessions, many of which were wedding gifts, was a depressing task. It was only a few months previously that they shared the excitement of moving in and starting their new lives together. Now all that they had planned, all their hopes and dreams were on hold. They did their best to stay positive, reminding each other of their dreams for the future together and of God's plan and provision they believed would carry them through. Betty's heart was fearful and heavy driving Paul to the train station. There were a great many tearful goodbyes on the station platform that day; they were not alone. After not enough hugs and kisses and promises to write every day, Betty watched the train until it disappeared then cried the whole way home.

Glenn reported to a base in Catonsville, Maryland where he became the chaplain's assistant. His duties kept him in the United States during his entire enlistment so he never had the anxiety of actually going overseas.

Paul was sent to Fort Polk, Louisiana for 16 weeks of basic training. The first eight weeks were tough, with the physical demands of getting into the shape the United States Army required of its soldiers. Then there was the adjustment to what the Army considered food, mostly mass produced, slightly tasteless but eatable. It did not come close to the meals his new bride had prepared for him. The Army served something it called chicken, but it resembled nothing Paul had ever seen in his life under the category of food and looked sickly lying on the shiny metal tray. Still, he was not one to complain, as there had been times when he was a boy during the Depression that his family would have been glad for even unsightly chicken. At least helping in the kitchen had prepared him for those occasions when he had KP duty, unlike those men who had never stepped into a kitchen in their lives. Early mornings, long runs and calisthenics, the constant barking of the drill sergeants and the bed at night that had seen better days blurred into a familiar routine.

The second eight weeks intensified from tough to extremely difficult when the training shifted to the combat skills the men would need for battle. Weapons instruction and hand-to-hand drills left no doubt in the recruits' minds that they were preparing to defend themselves, attack with force and know how to kill the enemy if necessary.

During this time of basic training, Paul met Privates Harry Sharff and Dale Seng. The three men were destined to become good friends later in Japan. For the present, they were just fellow new recruits hoping to live through the grueling weeks of training.

After basics, the soldiers were granted a very welcome two-week leave, during which time Paul and Betty went to New York City for a little getaway. They did their best to enjoy what time they had together and make the most of it. However, the reality that it was just a short respite between his enlistment and the next stopover was a cloud that hung over them. They were reminded of the pain of separation when they were in a soda shop on Times Square sharing a chocolate shake. Their hands touched on the glass when they leaned forward to suck the straws and Paul felt the ring on her hand that he still considered one of his most successful purchases.

"Would you have still married me, if I had been drafted before our wedding?" Paul asked Betty, looking across into those eyes that he knew so well.

"I would marry you again and anytime and anywhere you wanted," she replied. But that only made her tear up because they were a few days away from him leaving her again.

When his leave was up, they were once again on a train platform where she sent him off to Fort Lewis, Washington. It was known that the base was a major training and deployment center for those heading off to Japan and

Korea and Private Paul Nevel was scheduled to board a ship for Japan. They endured another tearful goodbye; Paul left on his train and Betty drove back to her parents' house, which was once again home for her.

Having grown up on dry land with no experience on a large body of water, the voyage to Asia introduced Paul to the horrors of seasickness, two straight weeks of it. The Army was hardly sympathetic; gut checks were all part of military service. The on-board doctor suggested plenty of fresh air. Well, walking on deck made getting sick over the side of the ship easier, just another gift to the sea. Pure agony was when he had nothing in his stomach which made staying hydrated important. Water, at least, came up easier than nothing. A sailor on the ship claimed that it was all in his mind. Ha! Paul knew better. It was in his stomach then it was not in his stomach, simple mathematics, not psychiatry.

It was hard enough to leave loved ones behind when someone made a choice to volunteer to serve in the military, as in the case of the modern U.S. military, but being drafted was far more difficult because those involved had little say in the matter. Add to the angst of being forced to leave their homes and interrupt their lives was the heartache of those left behind; fiancées, new wives and babies or young children. It tested the very mettle of the men ordered to serve their country. Boot camp was hard enough. It separated the men from the boys, or more accurately perhaps, it turned boys into men. Beyond basic training, each new soldier faced the unknown. One final difficulty was the nature of the Korean War. Few in America understood the complexities of world politics which made President Truman and other leaders in Washington feel the need to fight in a faraway land in a conflict few thought was their concern. Yet, these were the children of the Greatest Generation that had fought the Second World War against the Nazis and the Japanese, so they would do their duty as their parents had done theirs.

In Japan, Paul was assigned to Company B, First Battalion, 34th Regiment of the 24th Infantry Division. At the first chapel service held after his arrival on the base, he discovered that Harry and Dale from his boot camp class of recruits were also part of his new unit. Familiar faces were welcome in a place where everything else was new and different.

Dale was a jolly kind of fellow, a bit round in the middle, with dark hair and glasses. His good-natured humor and warm-hearted way of making people laugh reminded Paul of Glenn. Harry was tall and thin with lighter hair and a fair complexion, a spirit of kindness and a heart of gold. Paul knew these were the kind of men he wanted to be around, especially in this far away foreign land and amongst so much of the rough, sometimes vulgar, but mostly unsettling characteristics of many of the soldiers in his company. The unlikely mix of the draft, the war, music and faith drew the three men together to form a fast friendship that would grow and last a lifetime.

Talking about the women they left back home was a normal subject. It was a way to remain connected to their loved ones.

"Let's see a picture of her, Paul. Bet she can't match my pretty Elaine," Dale said when they first started to share about their private lives.

"I'll show you a picture, Dale, but remember she's taken," joked Paul.

He and Betty had several photos taken and developed at the Five and Dime before he left. He chose several of his favorites and carried them in his wallet.

"Ooh-weee, she is a doll!" exclaimed Dale. "Almost a match for Elaine, not quite, but you're a lucky man."

"I told you so," sighed Paul, which he always did when he took out the pictures and remembered the woman in them. "And yes, your Elaine is pretty, too."

Dale gazed at his photo of Elaine and, for a moment, he was home in Allentown, Pennsylvania; the weather was mild, the sun shining and he was at peace.

Harry chimed in, "What did either of you knuckleheads do to deserve such lovely girls? Let me show you my sweetie, Ann. She beats all." He pulled out a picture of a lovely young lady in a wedding gown with the afterglow of having just married the man of her life.

Paul nodded, "Very nice. How long have you been married?"

Harry tugged on a chain and pulled a gold pocket watch out of his pocket. He clicked it open, examined it briefly, put his finger to his cheek and squinted an eye for a second, as if he was thinking hard. "Three weeks, two days, eight hours and…" he consulted the watch, "48 minutes."

Paul laughed. "You mean to tell me you got married after we left boot camp?"

"Practically ran from my wedding to catch the last boat to…Japan," quipped Harry.

"Wow, and I thought I was a newlywed! You're a newly-wedded newlywed."

Looking at the black and white photo, Harry was dreamily back on the day of his marriage to Ann. "Yes I am. We are. I couldn't risk letting her get away while I was across the ocean."

"Smart man, smart man, indeed," Dale said with a wink. Harry chuckled, "Yes sir-y. Like I told Ann, I married her for money."

What? The other two soldiers looked at each other then at Harry.

"Um, a rich father or grandfather or something?" wondered Paul out loud.

"No," retorted Harry. "Or, not that I know of."

He looked at the surprised faces of the other men and shook his head in amusement. "Didn't you know that married guys make more from the Army than the single ones? As you know, Dale, a single soldier is paid 80 bucks a month." He wagged his finger at them like a pastor delivering a sermon, "Now a married man, of which I am one, is paid $40 a month but an $80 allotment is sent to his wife."

Nodding, Dale added, "Like I said, smart man indeed!"

The post-war late 40s and early 50s saw women leave the factories and other jobs they took while the men were at war to become wives, mothers and housewives. The job market for women returned to mainly those who were single. However, young wives of service men without children were treated in some respects as though they were single. Many took jobs back home while their husbands were deployed overseas and were able to put that allotment aside in the bank as a savings for their futures. Such was the case with the wives of Paul, Dale and Harry. The little nest eggs would later allow them to buy homes and start families when their husbands returned.

As the friendship between the three comrades grew, they shared a lot about their lives prior to the draft, talked about their wives and families, and supported one another through the difficult days of training for deployment to Korea and bouts of homesickness.

Company B, First Battalion, 34th Regiment of the 24th Infantry Division was initially stationed at a facility called Camp Fuji because of its location at the base of Mount Fuji, Japan. The mountain rose high and was the backdrop for every part of a soldier's stay. The base was part of those military

installations taken over by the United States military following World War
II and had a long history of military use. Samurai warriors had trained there
as early as 1198 AD and the Japanese army used the base extensively over
the centuries.

The training at the camp was the most rigorous any of the men had yet
experienced. They pushed hard, fully expecting that their next destination
would be in a combat zone. There were early mornings and long days, more
screaming sergeants and sore muscles. Not only were they trained for physical
endurance, but for mental toughness as well. The drills were designed to
prepare them to shoot weapons, carry heavy guns, ammo and backpacks
up, down and through the dense mountain terrain. The constant message
was to expect the unexpected and always be on their guards. Chow time
never came soon enough and their time in the rack was never long enough.
Instructors experienced in combat were determined to recreate as close to
the conditions of battle as was possible, which included fatigue in mind and
body and live fire drills.

When Paul was awake or had the opportunity before he went to sleep,
he would pull out his pen and paper and write to Betty by the light of the
dim barrack oil lamps. It was the tenor of his letters to not sound too sad
and resist writing about things which might worry her.

One typical letter said:

Dear Betty,
You'll be pleased to know I'm making some good friends here. Dale
and Harry are a lot of fun and are good Christian guys. You would
like them. We all joined the choir. It makes it a little less lonely, but
I miss you like crazy. They're both from Pennsylvania; Dale is from
Allentown and Harry from Philadelphia. Maybe we'll be able to keep
in touch after we get back home. They asked to see your picture, so
we all shared pictures and some stories after the chapel service today.
It felt good to laugh.

Their wives are pretty, but don't hold a candle to you. Still waiting
for our orders as to what comes next. For now, we spend the days
training and doing various drills. It's tough, but I'm hanging in there.
Have to sleep now, morning Reveille comes early. I'm glad I played the

clarinet and not the bugle...I'd hate to be the guy who gets everyone up! Hope I have sweet dreams of you. I love you, Paul.

Mail call was not just Paul's favorite time of the day; it was for every soldier. He, Dale and Harry would sit together and read their letters from home. As much as possible, they shared the news from home with each other. Of course, there were those parts of the letters a real gentleman just did not read out loud and that was understood with a wink and nod and a bit of friendly jealousy. Each letter from his wife that Paul received and held was almost like seeing and touching Betty, almost. Nevertheless, they were the force that kept him going.

Back in Altoona, Pennsylvania, Betty busied herself with work, church activities, time with family and lots of letter writing. Buck was a painter by trade and he thought it would cheer up his dear daughter to paint Paul's '34 Plymouth. They chose a color they thought Paul would like, a light green. Considering Paul was colorblind, Betty knew the lighter color would at least stand out to him.

Her family planned various activities so that Betty would have things to look forward to. But she did not look forward to anything quite as much as getting home after work and checking the mail every day. Being far away was hard enough when Paul was in the same country, let alone when he was overseas. She worried while he was on the ship, but tried not to worry. She worried about his days of military training in Japan, but tried not to think about what might happen or what could go wrong. And she worried about where his company would be sent when the training was over, but tried very hard not to think about it. Even though there was a lag of several days from when he posted the letters until she received them, she had a sense of relief with each one that he was fine and well and unharmed. They both wrote many a love letter during those months and though the postal service often seemed slow and uncertain at times, writing and receiving letters helped to get her through each day.

The other thing Betty looked forward to getting in the mail was her military allotment check from the government, which she would always take directly to the bank and put into their savings account. It was another connection to Paul, a tangible reminder that brought some comfort to her heart, thinking of better days to come and the future they would build together with the funds.

Neither of them realized that they would be seeing each other sooner than expected.

Two and a half months after his deployment to Japan, Paul received the devastating news. His father had sustained a severe blow to the head in an accident in the railroad shop where he worked. Soon after the accident, he suffered a cerebral hemorrhage as a result of the injury. His prognosis was not favorable.

Meanwhile, Harry's army experience also took a turn for the worse. Before being drafted, he worked for the telephone company in Philadelphia. In an unusual twist, the Army actually took advantage of his expertise. In June of 1952, he was running telephone wire through rice paddies, for communications between the company commanders and the battalion regiments. These were the same rice paddies where the men on latrine duty would dump human waste as fertilizer from a wagon hitched to an ox. One day, Harry noticed that he had a small puncture wound on his thumb. He didn't think much of it until he later saw a red line going from his thumb up his arm. He showed Dale when they returned to the barracks.

Dale was immediately concerned and said, "I think you'd better go see the medic, Harry. That doesn't look good; better safe than sorry."

The medic initially diagnosed him with a case of poison ivy but Harry was pretty sure that was not the case and sought another opinion, which saved his life and resulted in a one-week stay in the hospital. He had blood poisoning.

When Dale went to visit him and bring some cheer, he found a pale and sickly man.

A few days later Dale was back again to check on him and this time found his friend's condition much improved. "You're looking better, Pal, getting your color back. Not quite as green as you were last time I saw you," Dale said lightheartedly.

When Harry asked why Paul did not come with him, Dale sighed, "Paul's leaving today. He got a call that his dad was in an accident at work and now is in a coma. From what they're saying, it doesn't look good. He wanted me to let you know that he sends his get well wishes and prayers, but that's why he won't get to visit you."

Harry shook his head, "It's just like Paul to be thinking of someone else at a time like this. Did you ask if we could be stowaways in his luggage?"

Dale chuckled, as he had the same thought and replied, "I wish. At least he gets to fly. Let's pray he makes it home before his dad passes."

For many men in the military, the experience was the same. They became buddies with the guys next to them on the uncomfortable cots in the barracks or in the cold, wet foxholes. Those with whom they shared the hardships of training, deployment and combat became lifelong friends and men for whom they would give their lives, or at least the shirts off their backs. Their personal pain was nothing when compared with the needs of their comrades-in-arms.

Thanks to the Red Cross, Paul arrived home and, though it was a bittersweet homecoming, he did get to see his father while he was still alive. Unfortunately, James Nevel passed away soon thereafter. No one could believe James was gone at such a young age, he was just 41. Paul was given a month's leave and he was thankful he could be with his mother and siblings during this difficult time. Though only 21 years of age, he was the eldest of the children in his family and that meant the leader of the family. It fell to him to help his mother handle all of the arrangements before and after the funeral. For the third special occasion in his life, Paul wore his gray Gabardine suit, only this time it did not feel special. Although Betty was pleased with how the Army had sculptured her husband's muscles and thought he looked handsome all dressed up, he did not feel handsome. He merely felt the hurt in his heart, but now he was the man of the family, so he held his chin up and endured the pain.

How the young man dealt with such a radical change in his life was a testimony to his Christian faith and the love of a wonderful wife. Betty was his rock and comfort. It was for the couple another lesson in how marriage between two partners was meant to be, despite the difficulty of the situation.

The funeral was on the 4th of July. While the nation celebrated its birthday, the Nevel family and friends mourned their loss, entrusting James to his heavenly home with God.

Then with what the world would call fate or luck but what Paul and Betty believed to be divine intervention, God stepped in.

The headlines of the newspapers on July 27, 1953 read like a miracle taken directly from the Holy Bible: "TRUCE SIGNED!" and "WAR HALTS." Some of the sub headlines declared "Three Years Firing to End at 6 a.m." and "Big Guns Blast Until End, Yanks Die in Final Hours."

Many gathered around their radios to hear the news and latest updates; the war was over. Or, more correctly, was on hold. A ceasefire had been negotiated with North Korea. A line had been drawn and it would soon become famous in its own right; the Korean Demilitarized Zone (DMZ) running near the 38th parallel, covering roughly 248 kilometers between the two countries.

There was great rejoicing across the country over the war's end, while at the same time, grieving in much of the nation for the casualties of the war. More than 33,000 American troops died in combat, thousands more were killed in incidents related to the war. Another almost 100,000 were wounded and many of them would live the rest of their lives with the after effects of their wounds.

Betty's biggest concern was what it all meant for her husband.

Not long after Paul left for home in the United States and before the end of hostilities was announced, his unit was moved from Japan to Korea and the war zone. Harry, Dale and their company entered South Korea and headed north to a position near the front lines. From their camp, they could hear the heavy artillery, the swish of an outgoing round then the distant boom as it hit and the whoosh of incoming shells followed by the explosions that shook the ground. They were in reserve supporting the combat units facing the enemy. Nerves were on edge and adrenaline flowed while they awaited their turn to move up.

In the meantime, United Nations Command officials were at the table with the Communist leaders of North Korea trying to strike a deal. It finally happened. A cease-fire was agreed upon. At exactly 10 p.m. on July 27th an eerie calm fell over the battlefield of Korea.

Harry and Dale were in a foxhole on night watch when the truce was signed. It was getting close to midnight when Harry looked at Dale and whispered, "Do you hear that?"

Dale glanced into the night, afraid his friend had heard something very bad, and whispered back, "Hear what? I don't hear anything."

"That's the point," responded Harry.

The silence echoed through the dark valley.

The two soldiers, like many up and down the lines that night, kept waiting for it to resume, the popping, the explosions, the booming. But…nothing.

"Maybe this is it! Maybe it's for real — a cease fire!"

Rumors were a staple of Army life and, though hopeful, the two infantrymen knew the quiet could all be a rouse by the enemy. Then the word traveled quickly through the camp. Their sergeant validated their suspicions on his rounds, crawling past their hole. No more artillery. No more fear of ambush or snipers. A cease-fire had been agreed upon that day and was now in force.

But before he moved on, the sergeant advised his sentries to stay awake and stay alert.

The Korean Armistice Agreement signed in Panmunjom was more a cessation of hostilities than a peace treaty. It meant only that the two sides would stop shooting at each other and attacking across the manufactured boundary that became the 38th parallel. Some historians credit the dropping of the atomic bombs on Japan during the Second World War for helping to bring the conflict to an end, as North Korea knew the United States had the power to do it again.

Back in the United States, there was the question of how the war's end would affect Paul.

All too soon, his leave was officially over and he would be recalled to his unit. However, he learned that he could submit a request for an honorable discharge given the circumstances of his father's death, since his mother was now a widow, he was the eldest son in the family and there were still children at home. Paul, Betty and all their family and friends were hopeful that it would be approved, though in the meantime, Paul still had to report back to the Army for duty.

EIGHT

In September of 1953, Paul was sent to Camp Stoneman in California to what was called a replacement depot. There he would wait while the Army determined whether or not he would be discharged. A week went by, then two, then three. All the while, Paul was lonely and grieving over the loss of his father. He was tending to mostly mindless duties that were assigned to him, writing letters to Betty and just waiting. At a transitory camp, people came and went on a regular basis so there were few opportunities to make friends.

A month had passed when he finally received an envelope that he knew held the answer. He nervously tore it open, unfolded the typed letter and read the words "honorable discharge denied." He felt as if his heart sank to his toes. He dreaded making that call to Betty and his mother to let them know the bad news.

He calculated the time change to determine when Betty would be home after work and waited in line for the phone. When it was his turn, he slowly dialed the number to her parents' house. Betty heard the phone ringing and came running to pick it up. Something told her it was Paul.

"Hello?"

"Hi honey." Paul was not sure how his voice should sound. Even at that moment, all that he could think about was how the news would affect his wife, his love. He pictured her in his mind on the other end of the phone.

"Oh Paul, I was hoping it was you. How are you? Did you hear yet if you can come back home?" It all poured out of Betty.

Then there was silence, followed by Paul's halting voice, "It's not good news, sweetheart. I'm so sorry, so very sorry."

"Oh no, honey, tell me it's not true. We prayed so hard!" Betty said as she choked back tears. "We need you here. Your mom needs you here!"

One of the true mysteries of the universe is the divine will of God. In faith, Paul and Betty prayed that God would give them the desires of their hearts. They fully expected a miracle and could not conceive that He might say no. And yet, He had done just that.

"I know, Betty, I know. I tried my best and went through the proper channels. I have no other options. I guess they still need a lot of troops over there until things are stabilized. I'm so sorry, my love, so sorry."

There with her daughter, Mother Betty saw the expression on her daughter's face as the younger woman shook her head. Knowing what the expression meant, she walked away to give Betty privacy with her husband.

Outside the house, Buck Myers was arriving home from work.

"They won't discharge Paul, Buck," she said solemnly. "Looks like we'll have our little girl with us for a while yet."

"Oh no, my poor little Betty," said Buck. "Sure like having her around, but I know she had her hopes up for him to come home soon."

He walked into the dining room where Betty was standing beside the desk, just in time to see her drop the phone into its cradle and crumple into a chair with her hands covering her face. He walked over behind her and put his hands on her shoulders.

"Not good news, huh?"

"No, Dad, they won't let him go. He'll be going all the way to Korea in a matter of days. No telling for how long."

"I'm so sorry, sweet girl. We're gonna get through this, ya hear? You can continue to stay here in the attic room and save your money and the time will pass quickly, you'll see."

"I just feel so badly for him. Imagine…he just lost his father and his mom is heartsick and left to take care of the other kids on her own. It all just seems so unfair."

Taking her hankie from her sleeve, she dabbed around her eyes and blew her nose.

"Yes it does seem unfair. I'm afraid life isn't fair. War isn't fair. There are a lot of wives who are in your position and worse, wives who will never see their husbands come home. At least the war is over. He won't be going to the front lines."

"Yes, thank the Lord for that, at least," she agreed.

Her father continued, "Things happen for a reason and, yes, he's needed here, but he must be needed there, too. Paul is a good man and he loves you. He's called to a noble position, to fight for our country and I know he considers it an honor."

Her mother returned and the three hugged.

"He's strong and his faith is strong and he'll be okay," said Buck softly. "You know I wouldn't have walked you down the aisle and given you away to someone I didn't have faith in. And you have us."

Just then, Marlene walked through the door and the family hug was complete.

In California, Paul hung up the phone and just sat there for a moment in deep thought, still feeling stunned and letting the sadness wash over him.

"Hey buddy, my turn!" someone called out, startling him from his thoughts.

Looking around, he remembered that there was a line of men behind him all waiting for a phone.

"Okay, okay, it's all yours."

He sadly walked away and returned to his duties for the day. His orders had him sailing back across the ocean in just two days. Only this time, he would be headed for Korea and not Japan, not that it lessened the anticipated repercussions of sea travel. How he dreaded the thought of another bout with seasickness.

He talked about it with a couple of other men on their way back to the barracks that evening. The abrupt change in the Korean conflict had created an uncertainty in the ranks of the military. Right up to the signing of the cease-fire, the upper echelon had been preparing as though the war would continue. In a matter of weeks, when it became apparent that the halt in combat would be sustained, the military had to shift to a peacetime posture once again. Paul was surrounded by those in similar situations. There was confusion and many who had been drafted simply wanted to return to civilian life.

"I know it could be worse. I suppose I have to look at the bright side." He paused and gazed at the sun just before it disappeared behind a long gray building, leaving magnificent streaks of orange and yellow in its wake. The sky always reminded Paul of an all-powerful God who was so big and creative that He could paint a spectacular view like this. Yet, at the same time, God cared about him, his concerns and welfare. "Thank the good Lord the war is over and just in time or I could be going from here directly to the front lines with my unit. God spared us."

Since they were not going to solve the problems of the universe that night, the others moved on and Paul remained there watching the colors move and change, then dissipate into dusk. Against the magnificence of the Creator, he came to a decision.

"Dear Lord, give me strength to be the man You want me to be. I ask You to comfort my mom and Jake, Susie, and little Tommy. And please watch over my Betty and bring us back together again soon. If I can't go home, I guess you want me in Korea. At least I can join my unit and be with the guys I know."

He thought for a moment and decided there was something he would really, really like God to do for him.

"And Lord," he continued to pray, "if it's not asking too much, could You help me out and give my ship calm seas for the journey? Thanks for listening. Oh and thanks for the sunset to lift my spirits a little tonight. Amen."

In fact, the second sea voyage of Paul Nevel was a vast improvement over the first. There was some mild nausea but his trips to the head or the side of the ship were less frequent. Nevertheless, he would never be a seaman in anyone's navy.

When he arrived in Korea, it was his first taste of a dismal land, where winter brought freezing temperatures, frost bite, frozen equipment and heavy snow in which it was difficult to maneuver. Then there was summer with its drought and dense humidity which caused disease to spread and rats to flourish. Monsoon season flooded trenches and dug outs. Hilly, rugged terrain added to the difficulty of moving troops. Its saving grace was the Korean people. Those the American troops were fighting for and trying to protect were kind to them and respectful.

First things first, Paul was so glad to see his buddies. Climbing down from the Army cargo truck called the Deuce and a Half, in camp for the first time, he was excited to be reunited with Dale and Harry.

"We didn't know if you'd skipped out for good or not!" Dale said as he slapped Paul on the back. "Sure is good to see you. You'll have to get back in shape now, after being spoiled by your wife's cooking, no doubt."

Harry reached out to hug his friend. "So sorry about your dad, buddy. Have been praying for you and yours. Hope all went well, at least as good as can be expected."

Paul was weary from the travel and became a little misty-eyed. "It was hard to say good-bye to my dad. Never expected to lose him so soon, so young. Then leaving my mom, sister and brothers…really hard. And of course, Betty…"

The two comrades grabbed his duffel bag and they headed toward the barracks where most troops were housed except for those posted along the new border.

"Man, I don't know what to say, that's just tough all around."

"Yeah," said Dale. "Very sad and my heart goes out to you. You're gonna be ok, the good Lord must've brought you back here for a reason. At least you have us."

In later years, Paul would be able to reflect on the experience. Being sent back to his company, reuniting with Dale and Harry and serving in Korea beside them sealed friendships he might not otherwise have had. God's mysterious hand was on him. For at that moment, Paul was not privy to the plan of God in giving him two great gifts he would have the rest of his life.

"Yep, sure am glad for that," he sighed.

Harry brightened, "And you got here just in time for Dale's birthday."

"Now that's something to come all the way to Korea for," grinned Dale. "Oh and the choir, we've already decided for you that you'll be joining the choir. We have practice tonight."

"We even have choir robes, if you can believe that," Harry told him proudly.

In the barracks, Paul met familiar guys from his company and other units.

Over the next few weeks, he settled into the routine of a peacetime army near a potentially dangerous zone.

He discovered that Harry had an 8mm movie camera and the guys had fun using it. Paul thought he would like the idea of owning one, too. He bought an American made camera at the base PX and wrote to Glenn about finding a Kodak projector he could order for Betty from his base in Maryland. Glenn happily obliged and sent it on to Altoona.

Paul wrote to his wife, "This will be even better than letters, Betty, and better than pictures. I can record and send you the films to show you where we are, some of the things we're doing and the guys in my unit. I don't want you to forget what I look like! I carry your picture with me everywhere I go. In fact, I had a Korean artist paint your picture on a larger piece of paper and it turned out so good. Wish I could see the real thing, but for now pictures and movies will at least help."

And so Paul Nevel joined Harry Sharff and became a hobbyist cameraman, documenting some of the life of Company B, First Battalion, 34th Regiment of the 24th Infantry Division, but mostly how much he loved and missed his wife. In one note to her on the back of a photograph of him in his fatigues he wrote, "Paul Nevel, prisoner of love and of the Army."

One contentious issue of the armistice the adversaries had argued back and forth about was what to do with the prisoners of war (POWs). Some of the North Korean prisoners wanted to stay in the South to be free of communist rule. North Korea and China wanted to force them back to their countries, but the United States and their United Nation (UN) allies thought they should have a choice. This was part of the peace talks that lasted for more than two years. Finally, the North gave in and the agreement allowed the POWs to go where they wanted. Still, there were POWs to be moved. Over time, the UN repatriated, that is sent back to their own country, over 75,000 POWs, while the communist side returned under 13,000 POWs. Of that number only 8,726 South Koreans were returned, less than 10% of the total South Koreans who were MIA (missing in action). In one of their penetrations north during the conflict, UN troops found a mass grave of over 100 executed American prisoners which went underreported at the time. There were indications of war crimes, other mass executions of prisoners and brainwashing of prisoners with the communist ideals and then turning them into soldiers for the North.

Paul's unit was called on to play a role in prisoner exchange and they were moved to Pusan. The UN forces in South Korea had already begun the exchange before Paul rejoined his unit in Korea. When one of the POW camps was completely vacated, the Army converted those buildings into barracks where Company B stayed for the next six months.

"It's better than tents for the winter, gentlemen," was the word from their sergeant, a tough old bird who had seen his share of unpleasant duty.

Sure, it was not so bad if they could forget that the building paper lining the walls had been torn out to get rid of the bugs.

Always trying to lighten the mood, Dale quipped, "What a lovely hotel we have here, I wonder if we can get room service?"

Their responsibility in the prisoner exchange was to move the POWs from UN camps into trains that would take them north. Many would be moved to Formosa, which later became Taiwan. For the most part, it was peaceful if everyone followed the procedure. Once in a while a POW would resist, just out of spite for their American enemies, and force would have to be used to get him under control. But since the Korean and Chinese prisoners had a choice in where they wanted to be sent and since any difficulty they presented would precipitate a number of loaded M-1 rifles aimed at them in a moment's notice, there wasn't much cause for rebellion at this point. At least this duty was not boring or mundane. There were always new faces to see and the soldiers had to be vigilant and efficient in moving the prisoners.

When not on duty, the choir was definitely a good outlet and a morale booster. It sometimes caused tension with the master sergeant who was a macho man and did not like the choir guys or "choir boys" as he called them. However, the sergeant was overruled by the colonel who liked the music, so the choir continued. Also, being in the choir excused those involved from Sunday marching. They even convinced some Korean women to join them a few times and had enough robes to go around. The three friends also joined the Regimental Chorus, which was a smaller group that sang popular songs from Broadway and radio hits. They had a lot of fun with it and the troops enjoyed being entertained.

An army in a peacetime mode reverts to drilling when the troops are not otherwise engaged. That meant a return to physical training. When they were not assigned to specific duties, Paul's unit would spend the day in weapons training or sometimes it was marching...just marching and marching and marching. In the middle of running through the rice paddies one day in the valley between massive hills, someone shouted out in defiance, "Why the heck don't you just have us run up that hill?"

Big mistake. The sergeant in charge called out, "Column right!" And up they went.

Later in the mess hall, not only were all the soldiers famished but they were ready to kill the private who afforded them the opportunity to make the uphill run. The idiot that had to open his big mouth was smart enough not to admit to his stupidity and no one snitched on him.

The perceived pointlessness of the training for men who began to believe that they were no longer needed caused Paul to constantly remind himself and his pals to focus on the positives in the midst of so much negativity. It helped him to write letters home and dream about the future when he could return and pick up where he and Betty had left off. He read and re-read the letters from Betty and his mom, read his small pocket New Testament that he kept by his cot and tried to always give thanks in his prayers. Some days it was easier than others.

The North Korean and Chinese Armies and their Communist allies chased many of the civilians out of their cities during the conflict and into the South. They left in a hurry without anything to call their own but the clothes on their back and what they could carry. Families had been separated, and thousands of very poor displaced people were without homes, jobs or food. When the line was drawn at the 38th parallel to separate the North and South, they could not return to the North, and many destitute Koreans were left wandering in the area surrounding Pusan.

Paul's unit was involved in putting up makeshift tents to house refugee families. They would lay frames with wood for the floor, erect four corner posts, and lay canvas across the posts to provide shelter. There were so many it became like a tent city. There was a fence around the U.S. Army's compound and people would regularly come to the fence begging for food. Occasionally an officer would have a dog, but if the canine slipped out of the fence, it was rarely seen again. The refugees would snatch it up and the dog would end up as food. The displaced people would gather floating wood from the sea and dry it to cook any edible waste discarded near the military base. They had no pots or pans in which to cook over a fire so it was not uncommon for them to use stolen or discarded helmets. The M1 helmet was the standard issue combat headgear used by the military starting in World War II. It served multiple purposes and even the troops used them for boiling water and making coffee, cooking and shaving.

The Korean children especially tugged at the heartstrings of the American soldiers. If the GIs had chewing gum or candy on them when they walked anywhere outside of the compound, they would return with empty pockets. In desperation, some of the impoverished came up with creative ways to beg. Everyone knew about the blind man who played guitar with his guitar case open into which people threw coins or bills. Paul found out his blindness was a ploy one day when he offered some coins and the man reached out without groping to take them directly from his hand. Who could blame a man, not exactly blind but definitely poor. Paul paused for a moment, then winked at the man and let him have the coins. He never told the blind man's secret. Growing up without much in the Great Depression, before the Second World War, Paul knew what it was to be in want.

That is, he thought he did, until the war brought him to Korea where he saw the poorest of the poor and the desperation of a hungry mother looking for food for her children. It broke his heart.

Reflecting back, he would discover the subtle blessing of God in giving him sight to the world of want and need. Never, for the rest of his life, would he complain about what God chose to give him or not give him. He was blessed to live in his part of the world with his family and friends.

In November of 1953, a devastating fire swept through Pusan. Just when the American soldiers were longing to be home for Thanksgiving with their families eating turkey and the trimmings, they found themselves on the outskirts of the worst fire in Korea's history. Ripping through countless tent communities, homes and businesses, it did an unimaginable 40 million dollars of damage to the local economy. The Army aided the Red Cross in helping with relief efforts that left over 30,000 homeless. They housed 6,000 in an Army warehouse and offered 30-day rations to the homeless.

With Christmas drawing near, morale was low. The soldiers missed their families and simply wanted to go home. The Korean winter was cold and unrelenting, not to mention the Americans were surrounded by people in deplorable and what often seemed to be hopeless conditions.

Someone had the idea of throwing a Christmas party for the kids in a nearby orphanage. The sergeant saw the opportunity to improve the spirits of the men by giving them something to focus on. There was planning to do and logistics to work out; they had to secure enough food to serve a meal and locate presents for the children.

The day of the party arrived and they took the military transport trucks to the orphanage and loaded up the children in the back of the trucks. They were of all ages, all aglow in anticipation of the special treat. The orphanage had even managed to dress them for the occasion with anything red and green they could find. In Paul's opinion, the kids appeared better cared for than many of the kids he had seen on the streets. When the trucks arrived, he took out his 8mm camera and shot footage of the soldiers lifting the children out of the back of a truck and had one of the guys take a few shots of him doing the same. Then the children were taken to the tent where the party was waiting for them. What a special day it was. He loved seeing their smiling innocent faces and it was a gift in itself to be able to give something special to these children who were left as orphans in a war torn country.

Walking among the little ones, Paul dreamed of the day he and Betty would have children of their own. Reaching out, he touched their heads, looked at the smiles and caught the glimpse of the excitement in their eyes. He understood a little of what Jesus would have felt if He had been there surrounded by little children and perhaps Christ was in the person of His representative, Private Paul Nevel.

After Company B had wintered in the former POW camp, they moved northward to a camp originally constructed by the Imperialist Japanese Army during their occupation of the country. It was now called Camp George, named in honor of Private First Class Charles George of Cherokee Indian descent who was awarded the Medal of Honor for action in that area the year before. When they arrived, they set up tents which would be their living quarters, with nine men per tent. There were trenches for latrines and a spigot coming out of the ground for water. They bathed and washed clothes out by hand in a nearby river that flowed into the Pacific. The barracks with the bug wall paper did not seem so bad in comparison.

One day when Paul was stooped down washing out clothes in the rocky stream, Harry grabbed Paul's movie camera and thought this was something Betty should see.

"I'm gonna let Betty know you can take over the laundry responsibilities when you get home. Just give the guy a bar of soap and watch him go to town," he mocked Paul as he filmed.

Paul laughed. But the bar of soap slipped off the rock into the water. He reached down for it, laid it back on the rock and started scrubbing a stained white undershirt he was washing when the bar slipped into the water again. It occurred a few more times until Harry said, "Okay, cut. I think she'll get the idea. Slippery soap makes for a slippery slope. Maybe you could do a commercial for Army soap, 'Lean and mean scrubbin' it clean.'"

Paul was about to splash Harry with water, but just in time remembered it was his camera in his friend's hand. Later when they set up a projector to watch some of their footage, they laughed and gave Paul a hard time about his skill as a laundry service person. They were simple events of life and yet they cemented the friendships of these men.

Then Dale had an idea, "Try running that backwards."

As they watched in reverse, they laughed even harder when the soap appeared to leap from under the water and slide back up on the rock over and over, while Paul kept trying to place it on the rock to stay.

"I guess the sad state of affairs in Korea is such that we are easily amused!" Harry finally noted.

News of the progression of peace after the war continued to seem favorable. The Army had learned that it was beneficial to morale to give the soldiers a break away from the monotony of army life in the field and it made a world of difference in the attitude of the troops. R&R ("rest and recuperation" or "rest and relaxation" as some called it) was introduced into the routine of the various units. Knowing it was coming gave the GIs something to look forward to. They were pulled from their units and sent to Seoul or Japan and returned refreshed, more productive and ready to more efficiently do their duties. Not everyone was so lucky as to get R&R, but all were hopeful.

Paul, Harry and Dale were fortunate enough to be scheduled together in a group of twenty men from their unit sent on R&R to Japan. They were really looking forward to sleeping on a real bed with four walls around them, as opposed to on a cot in a tent. A bath or shower in an enclosed room would also be a welcomed luxury. They would find a local inn or hotel to stay in when they arrived in the country. After eating so much canned food and C-rations the past several months, they could not wait to sink their teeth into a juicy steak.

C-rations were provided by the U.S. Military when fresh food or mess halls or field kitchens were not available in which to prepare packaged food. The C-rations came in a box that the soldier would often open and eat from directly. Rations included crackers, beans, wieners, stews, and potted meats in a can. They also had gum, candy, and cigarettes for the smokers. Word from those who had gone on R&R before them said they would be greeted on the base in Japan with a hearty meal, a shower and a clean uniform.

The day before their departure, they found out that the Army had sent out all of the airplanes from their airport on a mission to Berlin, so their departure was delayed. Their hearts sank, afraid they had missed their chance. It was a disappointment, but someone at HQ managed to arrange alternative transportation. They were to be driven to the coast where they caught a boat to Japan.

"Oh, great," said Paul, a bit understated to the joyous response by Dale and Harry when they learned the news.

Fortunately for everyone, and Paul especially, the seas were calm and the trip was a few long hours and not days. Still, he did not fail to offer at least one prayer for a divine blessing.

From the moment they finally stepped off the boat in Japan until they left, the three soldiers made the most of every minute. They were first given that hearty breakfast of steak and eggs everyone raved about and thereafter ate at the PX or at a Japanese restaurant chosen from a list of those approved by the Army. Southern Japan where they were sent was a tourist area similar to Florida in that the weather was really hot and it was crowded in the summer. But since it was March and a little cooler, it was the perfect time to rent bikes and ride around the city. The young men from the heartland of America saw things their eyes had never seen. It was their opportunity to let their hair down, in the vernacular of the day, although all three men had army haircuts so letting down their hair was purely symbolic. They explored another culture and did as they pleased when they pleased. Oh, the freedom! It felt great to feel the wind in their faces as they raced down the street on their bikes and performed dare devil stunts, trying to outdo one another. They visited beautiful gardens and a park where there were amusement rides and monkeys roaming about. Paul even swung on the swings and had Harry film him with the movie camera, blowing a kiss to Betty as he jumped from the swing and executed a perfect landing. They took photographs of a large Buddhist temple and wandered through the markets along the streets selling everything from fresh fish to hand-made crafts and clothes. Of course, they had to buy souvenirs for their wives.

Paul found a beautiful hand-crafted jewelry box at one of the stands.

"Isn't this a thing of beauty? I think Betty would love it."

The outside of the box was overlaid with a shiny ebony lacquer, decorated with colored pictures of Japanese trees and flowers etched and inlayed with abalone shell. He carefully picked it up and found a little knob on the bottom that turned.

"Oh, it's a music box. Better yet."

He wound it a few times, opened the lid and it began to play the Blue Danube, a waltz often played when he and Betty would skate together. When he closed his eyes, he was back in Altoona with his love and they were taking another turn around Lakemont Park's Roller Arena, hand in hand. Initially the tune made him happy but then the thought of missing Betty gnawed at his insides and the good mood threatened to go away.

Fortunately, Harry snapped him out of his doldrums daydream, "Wow, that really took someone a lot of time to make; it's quite a work of art."

Oh yeah, Paul was back in the present and he examined it closer. The interior was lined with a blue velvety material with a diamond shaped mirror on the underside of the lid. Usually Paul would check a price on something to make sure it was a bargain or on sale before he considered making a purchase, but it was too late. He knew he was buying the music box for Betty, regardless of the cost. She was worth it.

Harry spotted a large wooden wagon full of goods being pulled not by a bike or a horse, but by what looked to be older Japanese women. "Look at that — I feel like we should go help them."

"Hold on," Dale stopped them. "I heard about this. When the Japanese women get to a certain age, they actually put them on road crew duty. It's their job."

"Seems a shame, looks like a man's work," said Harry.

Eventually, it was agreed that they should pay for the box and move on.

The best part of R&R was getting several good nights' sleep and feeling clean. All too soon their leave was over. Back to the grind they would go.

"Thanks for a great time, fellas," said Dale. "For now, it's 'sayōnara' to lovely Japan and carefree days. At least our time in Korea is winding down. That is if the Army doesn't throw us any surprises."

"Wouldn't it be great if our next R&R time was in home sweet home Pennsylvania?" Harry said wishfully. His wish came true, though it took another six months to complete their tour of duty.

After a few more months of hard work at and around the base, summer rolled around again with warmer days and improved morale among the troops of Paul's unit with the anticipation of their time in Korea coming to an end.

One sunny hot July afternoon, the assembly bugle call sounded to summon the troops to their designated gathering area by the flag pole in the compound. It was an unusual time for a general assembly, but they dared not question it out loud. Paul guessed it was a surprise inspection of some kind or there was breaking news to announce. Quickly they were in formation and were called to attention. They waited.

Then the staff sergeant appeared, pacing in front of the troops. The command was given, "At ease." They could move into a more relaxed position, hands clasped behind their backs, feet shoulder width apart, with upper body still in a position of attention, chest out and shoulders back.

"Gentlemen, you've been working diligently and carrying out your duties with respect to your commanders as well as your fellow soldiers and the Korean people you encounter outside the compound. I commend you for your tireless service. I know it's been a long road and we have required much from you. There are those of you who won't like what I'm about to say, but you know the consequences for complaining. I need you to go to your bunks, deflate your air mattresses, bring them and a change of boxers and report back here in 10. Dismissed!"

The men hustled to their barracks to gather their items, all abuzz with questions wondering where they were headed. "Are we sleeping outside tonight? What on earth is going on? Where are they taking us with no weapons?"

When they reported back to the flag pole, they were loaded onto transport trucks and off they went. It was a short drive to a sandy beach where the sergeant called them off the trucks and into formation.

He then ordered them to blow up their rubber mattresses, strip down to their boxers, and go ride some waves. They were being awarded a few hours of recreation.

There was a lot of swimming, splashing, dunking, laughter, catching waves on their mattresses and relaxing on the beach that afternoon. What a treat it was, much deserved and much enjoyed.

NINE

So as it was with her husband, war time for Betty Nevel was filled with highs and lows and small miracles from heaven by God's good grace. But while Paul had two buddies with whom to share the experiences, men who had the same frame of reference he did, Betty was alone even while surrounded by family and friends. For none of them knew what suffering she endured in the quiet of the nights when no one was there. No one could see into her thoughts when they ambushed her with visions of what could befall her husband while he was kept from her.

United States Army Privates Paul Nevel, Harry Sharff and Dale Seng experienced the sentiment of many who formed the military band of brothers, finding comradery and trust in one another as they went about their daily routines with the unit. When one man was struggling with homesickness or feeling down in the dumps, the others would rally around him with a timely word of encouragement or a pat on the back and something to make him laugh, or at least chuckle. Having a shared faith and sense of humor sure helped, aiding them in the ability to find the positives in hardships and things for which to be thankful in the midst of dismal surroundings. Without pretense, Paul, Harry and Dale gained the respect of their fellow soldiers and became role models among their peers. The other men in the unit knew if they needed a listening ear or some sound advice, they could go to any of the three. There is something about a light in the darkness that gives hope and draws people to its source.

One evening after reading a letter from Elaine, Dale said, "Ya know guys, I bet our wives would be good friends if they knew each other. Whadaya say we see if the three of them want to become pen pals?"

"I've thought the same thing," answered Harry. "They're probably going through a lot of similar stuff with us being away. It might be a really neat thing for them to connect."

Paul agreed. "Betty likes to write letters and send cards to people. I think she'd really enjoy getting to know the wives of the two buddies I've told her so much about."

"Wait a minute," insisted Dale. "What did you tell her about me?"

"Nothing to worry about," quipped Paul. "I didn't tell her anything that was the truth."

"Whew," Dale responded mockingly.

"I don't know," joked Harry. "You just might want to worry about that."

Many nights for Betty consisted of coming home from work, eating dinner with her family then heading to her room in the attic where she, hopefully, had a new letter from Paul to read. If not, she read an old one.

She would talk from time to time with her father and mother and with Marlene about what she was feeling but, it was not that they did not want to understand, they just could not. It was for her, a lonely war.

That all changed with a letter she received postmarked May 22, 1953 from Elaine Seng.

Elaine was Dale's wife and the first to catch the vision of comradeship their husbands had suggested from far-off Korea.

Dear Betty,

First, I want to introduce myself. I am Dale Seng's wife, Elaine. Dale had suggested that I write to you, so here I am. You know, there is something I am so thankful for, and that is that Dale has met so many wonderful fellows in the service, and one in particular, your Paul. Dale has talked an awful lot about Paul and how much alike their interests are. According to the way he writes and talks, it seems he has found his equal.

Now, I will tell you about myself. I am a stenographer. I work in an office of Charis Corporation. Sometimes I work on the switchboard. It is very interesting work.

Dale and I have an apartment consisting of two rooms and a private bath. We think it is very cute, too. We've been married two years and five months, and most of that time was spent in this apartment. I've

*given it a name – "The Abode of Everlasting Felicity." That is the way
I feel about it! Do you and Paul have an apartment, too?*

*We have our hearts set on owning a home and raising a family
of three or four children. We also love animals and Dale is certain to
have at least two dogs! He is the type of person who is loaded with
beautiful and wonderful original ideas. So we will be making use of
those wonderful ideas when he gets home and we can start making a
cozy and comfy home of the house we want to buy.*

*Some of my hobbies are: knitting, reading, sewing, cooking, music,
etc. I love to do things with my hands. I like working in the outdoors.
I should say, I love to do everything if Dale were with me.*

*Do you like music? Dale and I belong to the choir of our church
and like all kinds of music. It was hard for me to see Dale go last
December, just before all the festivities of Christmas. But I guess I
wasn't the only one like that.*

*It would be nice if you, Ann (Harry's wife) and I could get together
sometime this summer for a weekend here in Allentown. How about it?*

*I guess I'll close now and let's keep praying that God will protect
and guide our boys while they are away from us for the time being.
Also, I hope you and I will become good friends while we have one
thing in common, our boys. I hope too that you will write me soon
and let me know all about you and Paul. Until I hear from you,*

    Cheerio, Elaine

After reading the letter, Betty felt like she had looked into a mirror.

It warmed her heart to receive Elaine's letter and she promptly responded. Soon Ann Sharff joined the letter writing circle and the three women made plans to meet for a weekend in Allentown. Betty was farther away and traveled by train, Ann drove, and Elaine excitedly prepared her Abode of Everlasting Felicity for their arrival. It was friends at first sight and did not take long for them to feel comfortable talking and laughing together. Betty and Ann brought in their suitcases and Elaine put them in the spare room.

"Dinner will be ready in about twenty minutes. Hope you'll enjoy a good ole' Pennsylvania Dutch meal of chicken and dumplings," Elaine said, almost too excited to contain herself.

Unlike their husbands' first experience together in boot camp with the Army's version of chicken, Elaine was an outstanding cook and the chicken tasted very good and very much like chicken.

After the meal, they sat in the living room and talked for a couple of hours. They compared notes on what they had heard from their husbands, shared their worries, fears, and hopes for the future.

"Ann, I'm so glad Harry took his movie camera with him, because it encouraged Paul to get one," Betty remarked. "It brightens my days to get reels in the mail from time to time and to be able to see our husbands working and playing. Paul is always blowing kisses or holding up a piece of cardboard or something-or-other he found to scratch a note on, saying 'I love you' or 'Hi Betty'. I wish the movies had sound. I brought mine with me, in case we get a chance to watch them together."

Agreeing with her sentiments, Ann chuckled, "I brought my reels from Harry, too. And brought along our projector. Why don't we set it up and watch them together?"

Elaine was ecstatic. She had not been as fortunate as the other two ladies to see her husband since he left for Japan. "Oh that would be wonderful. I don't have a screen, though. Will that wall over there work?"

"Sure," said Ann and she went to the car to get her reels and Kodak reel-to-reel projector.

Elaine said, "Let's put on our pajamas and get comfy. I'll make the popcorn."

They settled in for the rest of the evening of nostalgia watching the movie reels, laughing and sharing more than a few tears. Being able to watch their men bond together created an even stronger bond among the three women. They finally had others who understood what they were experiencing.

The next day, Elaine showed them around Allentown and they did what close girlfriends often do together, they went shopping. In a dress boutique, while they perused the skirts and dresses, Ann had an idea.

"Wouldn't it be fun to get matching outfits and take pictures of us wearing them to send and surprise the boys?"

Betty and Elaine loved the idea. They giggled like schoolgirls and searched for just the right outfit then tried on a few options in the dressing room. They settled on a full circle swing dress, white with big red and blue polka dots, that was available in each of their sizes. As they walked to Elaine's car with their purchases, they were giddy with excitement.

Ann said, "This is so much fun! Wait until the boys see the three of us together in our matching patriotic dresses!"

"Now all we need is someone to take our photo," Betty added.

On Sunday, the ladies attended Elaine's church together. Elaine was glad the choir was not singing so she could sit with her friends instead of in the choir loft.

All too soon their weekend together came to an end.

"Parting is such sweet sorrow," Betty noted when she carried her suitcase to Ann's car. Ann was going to drop her off at the train station on her way home. "Sorrow because I'm sad to leave you two after such a fun time together and sweet because I have two new dear friends. For our next visit, it's your turn to come to Altoona!"

They all shared the feeling that this was the beginning of lasting friendships.

For Betty, she was no longer alone in the experience of having an Army husband far away in Korea. She, too, had war buddies.

On the train back to Altoona, she could not help but feel that God had truly blessed her in a very unique way.

TEN

Fall seemed to drag along for Company B which continued to patrol the area and carry out their postwar efforts. At least the cooler weather offered some relief. Paul sent Betty letters, pictures and movie reels when he could, and letters from her helped to keep him going.

The season also brought rumors that members of the First Battalion, 34th Regiment of the 24th Infantry Division were rotating home and most would be discharged. Though no one dared believe it, they all wanted to.

In October, Private Paul Nevel was the first in his unit to get his orders to report for discharge. He was never more ready to go home. He learned that his two trips across the ocean had earned him extra rotational points. Once again, God had reached out to touch his life in an unexpected way.

Though happy for him, the other men were envious and did not hold back giving him a rough time about it.

"You can't go away and leave us," insisted Harry.

"Hey, you should tell the Army you're not leaving your comrades behind," suggested Dale. "Either everyone goes home or you stay right here."

"I'll be sure to do that, Dale," Paul replied with a smile. "But first, I'll have to clear it with Betty."

Paul, Harry, Dale and the thousands of Americans and UN allied troops who served in the military during the Korean War were never the same following their tours. Paul was proud to have served his country and play a role in this critical conflict that was a turning point in the fight against communism. For many, the experience was also a turning point in a young person's life that was either good or bad. Fortunately, Paul was determined to see it all work together for good in his life. He had seen things he wished he never would have seen, but survived it all, and learned valuable lessons about courage, sacrifice, honor, responsibility, faith and life that could never be taken away.

The day had finally come; Paul was returning home, where he belonged. When he received his orders, he quickly sent word in the mail to Betty and his mom, knowing it was possible that he might just beat the letters home.

He bid Dale and Harry farewell after promising that they would look each other up once they were all back in Pennsylvania. And there were others with whom he had bonded who also wanted to stay in touch when they were safely stateside. On a cool October morning, Paul climbed into the back of a Deuce and a Half transport truck with the other fortunate GIs and watched his friends and Korea fade into the distance.

Nevertheless, he had one more battle to face; the horrible two week struggle with sea sickness on the voyage from Korea to California. Although he knew it would be worth it, the perpetual nausea was as horrible as he had remembered and he promised God all sorts of things if only He would grant him a small break from the churning stomach. It kept him going to know he would soon see Betty's face and wrap his arms around her. He was also very anxious to get back to check on his mother and siblings. They had not left his thoughts and prayers and he hated that he had to leave them at their time of need after his dad had passed away.

The transport ship was a huge, crowded vessel of some 4,000 people. It was like a whole city crammed into a big topsy-turvy metal container that somehow floated on the water. Well, floated was perhaps a generous word from Paul's perspective; it bobbed like a porpoise in and out of the water. Bunks were stacked anywhere from three to six men high and that was where he spent a lot of the voyage, with guys acting as angels of mercy bringing him saltine crackers, ginger and apples. Nothing helped a whole lot.

Word spread throughout the ship of the approach of the west coast of the United States. Soldiers rushed onto the deck and searched for the first signs of land. Even Paul managed to make his way out to join them. When they spotted the coastline, a big cheer went up. Paul could not wait to get his feet back on solid land and figured he would be one of those guys who knelt down and kissed the ground. When the ship sailed into San Francisco, they saw the famous Golden Gate Bridge and it was quite the sight to see.

They continued until they passed under the fascinating landmark, which at the time had the longest bridge span in the world.

When he finally put his feet on the ground in California, he thought he would never get his land legs back, not to mention his stomach. Happily, instead of a long train trip across the country, the Army put him on a plane to Fort Meade, Maryland. The flight was long, but much quicker than the other options. Once he arrived on the base, he had to read and sign a stack of paperwork, then wait on the Army's processing for several more days with little to do. When Glenn got word that Paul was only fifteen miles away from him, he could hardly get there fast enough. The two men were thrilled to see each other again and just catching up gave Paul something to do with himself.

That night, they opted to skip the mess hall and went off the base in search of a restaurant.

"What sounds good that you haven't had in Korea?" Glenn asked.

"Anything except for seafood," Paul said. "I'm still recovering from being seasick." It made Paul's stomach churn just to think of anything in the seafood family.

"Sorry to hear that, pal. You are truly a survivor of the war and of the sea. I know of a good steak place and it's next to the theatre, if we want to catch a flick after dinner," Glenn offered.

Paul responded, "Sounds great. So glad to be back in the good ole' U.S. of A."

They had a lot to talk about between bites as Paul savored a steak and baked potato, his first non-army meal in a long, long time.

It was then that he learned that Glenn's war was far different.

Even though he had to endure the physical aspects of boot camp, the hardest part for him was the book work and on the job training when he started down the road to being a chaplain's assistant. Then it became tougher when the troops came back before the ceasefire, some wounded in body and some in spirit. Some made it through recovery, some did not and some Glenn would never know what became of them. The core tenets of their mission were "nurturing the living, caring for the wounded, and honoring the fallen." "I've heard a lot of sad stories and sometimes it's just about listening and letting people get things off their chest," he told his cousin. "We also connect the soldiers with agencies that can help support them. You know how it is being away from home and in dangerous conditions. The guys come back different, some different in a positive way, some in a negative way. We just have to keep pointing people to hope, to God, to the great purpose and honor there is in serving our country."

In some ways, Paul considered that his cousin and friend had a much harder war.

Paul said, "So you're like a professional counselor now, huh?"

Glenn nodded. "Fetch me my white coat and call me doctor. Now if you'd like to lie down on the couch and tell me all of your woes..."

Through dinner and dessert, the two men reflected on how God had brought them through the difficult times away from home and they would soon be back in Altoona.

"I am stuffed," Glenn said. "That was a great meal. But I have to say the chocolate cake didn't compare to your wife's."

Paul agreed. "That's for sure. If I wasn't so full, my mouth would be watering at the thought of it. Still have time to make the movie?"

Glenn glancing at his watch said, "Yep, if we hurry."

It pleased Paul to see that Glenn had fared well since they had been apart and Glenn was so thankful his cousin had returned unharmed and stronger for the experience.

They ended the night at the cinema where they could turn off their brains, sit back and let the entertainment experience flood over them.

Instead of Paul taking the train, his brother Jake volunteered to drive to Maryland to pick Paul up at Fort Meade and drive him home. Jake asked their cousin John to join him and excitedly took off on the road trip in his '34 Plymouth. The car was a hand-me-down from Paul to his younger brother when he bought a '39 Plymouth. When they reached the base, it was a welcome reunion and Paul was all the more glad that his journey home was close to realization. They talked and laughed and also got a little misty-eyed reflecting on how the year had been for the family without their father. The men spent the night at the base and, as Jake would often quip later, it was the only night he ever spent in the Army. Paul was emotionally exhausted yet restless as he tried to sleep. His body was still recovering from those two rough weeks on the ocean and a long plane flight across the country. How he had waited and longed for this time to come and now it was here. Lying awake in his cot, he considered that, as excited as he was to see his bride face to face, he could not help but be a little nervous as well. All seemed fine in her letters, but two years was a long time to be apart. Would she be as eager to see him as he was to see her?

At the same time, Betty tossed and turned in her bed, trying to sleep, knowing she would have to get through work the next day. She had prayed every day for over a year for Paul's safe return and she could hardly believe she would finally see him. Her thoughts drifted from prayers of thanksgiving to trying to calm those crazy butterflies in her stomach and everywhere in between. She tried to push away worries, wondering if anything had changed or would feel different between them. The man who returned for his father's funeral was a changed man and that was only after a few months. Now over a year later, what would the man who came home be like?

The next morning with Paul's paperwork finalized, he bid the Army farewell and drove off the base on what would finally be the last leg of his journey home. Knowing Betty would not be off work until 5pm, Paul asked Jake to first take him to see their mother and family at the house where he grew up. His younger brother and sister were so excited and had hung a "Welcome Home Paul" banner they had made themselves across the front porch of the house.

When the car pulled up, they all ran to the door to greet him with giggles and hugs. So relieved to see her Paul home at long last, a weeping Murry Nevel held her son as if she feared by letting go he would leave her again. The young man she held so tightly was not the same as the boy who left for the Army so long ago or to whom she bid goodbye after her husband's funeral. That young naïve and possibly uncomplicated person was gone, replaced by a man who had matured through his wartime experiences.

At the Metropolitan Life Insurance Company, Betty was useless the entire day but did her best to do her job and not think of all the things that could delay the guys on the road. Her boss graciously let her leave an hour early and she walked out of the office to cheers and well wishes from her coworkers. She drove home and hurried into the house, calling to her parents as she ran up the stairs to her room to freshen up, "He'll be here soon."

Donning a new navy blue skirt and white blouse she had bought just for this occasion, she brushed her hair, powdered her nose, applied her favorite red lipstick and checked her appearance in the mirror. What else could she do? Was there something she could add to look better?

Too late, she heard a car pulling up and just knew who it was. She practically flew back down the stairs and missed one or two.

Outside, Jake's car was stopped in front of the house. It took a moment for Paul to realize the green car parked there was his '39 Plymouth. He thought he would be there to greet Betty when she returned home, but she was already home. Stepping out of the car, he was just in time to see her burst out the front door. He stood still for just a second; didn't the whole world stand still with him? Wow. Was that gorgeous young lady, dark curls blowing in the breeze, really his wife? His heart was going to pound out of his chest and he found himself trying to catch his breath when, suddenly, she ran to him. He swept her up in his arms and twirled her around. This was not a Hollywood film; it was real life in motion, two very real people in a very real love story.

He pulled back and looked into those familiar blue eyes and their lips met in a long-awaited kiss. Both of them felt at that moment, finally, all was right with the world.

After several minutes of hugs and kisses and excited chatter that neither actually heard as words just poured from them, they kissed again and held onto each other.

Jake and John moved Paul's bags to the porch where Buck and Betty Myers waited.

His mother-in-law greeted Paul with a warm hug. "Welcome home, Paul. You look good, a sight for sore eyes. Um, but you're a little thin. Did you get enough to eat over there?"

Buck shook his hand, probably a little firmer than he intended. "Glad to see you, young man, mighty glad. Bet you're happy to be back on U.S. soil. I'm sure you have some stories to tell! But that can come later. Let's get you settled in."

Buck took Paul's Army green duffel bag and walked it up the stairs to Betty's attic room. Paul followed him with his other bag. "I sure do appreciate you letting us stay here for a while, 'til we can get adjusted and on our feet a little."

"Aw, now, don't mention it. We wouldn't want you anywhere else. Well for now, that is," Buck winked at him.

By the time the men walked back down the stairs, Betty's mother was setting the table. "You must be hungry. C'mon now, sit down and have some dinner."

Paul pulled a chair out from the table, "Will you sit beside me, Mrs. Nevel?"

"Why I'd be honored to sit beside you, Soldier," a happy Mrs. Nevel replied.

That evening around the table at the Myers' house, the prayer for the meal was more than just something they did to ask God to bless the food and the hands that prepared it. It was a sincere thanks to the Lord for bringing home their son-in-law, the husband of their dear daughter Betty. They were, indeed, thankful to God.

ELEVEN

The next couple of months took some time for Paul to settle back into life in the U.S. and adjust to living in his in-laws' home with Betty. There were so many stories to tell, experiences to share, friends to visit, and just catching up on life in general. He had learned to take nothing for granted. Growing up in the Depression era, his parents had done their best to provide for their family, but they lived on very little. Seeing how other parts of the world had it even worse, far worse, just confirmed all he had to be thankful for. He would be careful to spend his money wisely and with frugality. Even a trip to the grocery store caused some reverse culture shock; it was hard to comprehend such surplus when all that came to mind was starving Koreans begging at the Army compound's fence.

One thing he planned to put some money toward was a trip to Florida for that real honeymoon he had promised Betty. He figured after being apart for so long, they both deserved the chance to be together and alone. Betty was looking forward to it. She had saved up vacation days and concurred with her husband that it was a wise investment, indeed.

A week after Paul returned home, he and Betty packed their bags for their great adventure. Betty was never fond of the idea of flying, and it made her nervous when Paul had to board a plane. She, for one, was glad it was more affordable to drive to Florida. It took two days to get there and they spent a night in a hotel on the way. The drive was a nice opportunity for them to catch up and to have some long-awaited time together. By driving, they could take in the scenery along the way, the changing vistas of the different states.

They had not driven too far out of town when Paul asked, "Were you nervous to see me, Betty?"

She paused. "Well, why…were you nervous to see me?"

He grinned and said, "I asked you first. Well…okay, I'll go first. Yes, I was nervous. It was a long time for us to be apart. I hoped and prayed you'd still feel the same for me and that nothing drastic had changed between us."

Betty put her hand on his knee, as she sat in the middle of the front seat as close to him as she could get. "Honey, I missed you like crazy, every day. Yes, I was nervous and felt the same way, wondering if anything would feel different between us. But I know now that I love you more than ever. It feels so good to have you back. And now we're on our way to our Florida honeymoon. It's just like I dreamed it would be."

Paul breathed a big sigh of relief. All indications were that all was well, but it felt good to hear her say it. "You know, at this moment, there's no place on earth I'd rather be than by your side in our Plymouth on a road trip to the tropics. I have to pinch myself to realize it's real."

Betty teased, "I can take care of that for you." Then she pinched his leg. He flinched. "Hey watch that, I'm driving!"

They laughed and she kissed his cheek. It was going to be a wonderful trip. They nestled in and watched America roll by outside their windows, thankful and content just to be together.

They planned to stay with Paul's Aunt Tonie, who was his mother Murry's youngest sister. Murry was short for Marilla and Tonie's given name was Iona. All of the girls in the fifteen Rudasill children had names that ended with "a" — a fun fact they liked to tell people as they listed all of the names. Tonie and her husband J.C. lived near Miami, Florida and had plenty of room for guests. They were thrilled to host Paul and Betty on their Florida get-away.

When they pulled into the driveway, Tonie ran out to greet them with a barrage of happy chatter, her three children in tow. "It's wonderful to see you kids! So glad you made it! How was the trip?"

"Well we're ready to be out of the car, that's for sure," exclaimed Paul. "Our new trusty Rand-McNally Atlas plus the directions you gave me over the phone served us pretty well. We didn't even get lost."

Betty gave him a side-ways look. "Paul...?"

Daniel Boone was purported to have said, "I ain't never been lost but there was a time when I was a mite bewildered for about three days."

Betty considered that her husband might be closely related to the American icon. Of course, they did share one trait, they were both men and everyone knew about men and asking for directions.

"Well, we didn't," Paul protested, "I always knew right where I was, in the car beside you."

They all had a laugh.

Betty said, "Okay, then, I won't tell them we got turned around a time or two and I had to talk you into stopping to ask for directions."

J.C. smiled as he slapped Paul on the back. "There's a good soldier for you. Trusting your inner compass. Or maybe you should've brought along your real compass?"

"Oh, the bliss of young love," remarked Tonie. "C'mon you two, let's go inside and get you settled in your honeymoon suite."

The 10 days in Florida proved to be a great vacation. They had some meals and outings with J.C. and Tonie and Paul's little cousins, including a couple of days at a nearby beach. Tonie also made sure the two love birds were given time to themselves. After all, it was their second honeymoon and she was keen to help make it a bit more romantic than the Young Adult Retreat weekend at Camp Christian. They visited some attractions such as "Monkey Jungle" where they saw tropical flora and birds, monkeys and alligators. It was advertised that you could watch a man wrestle an alligator. Unfortunately, they were disappointed to find out they arrived too late and just missed it.

Paul went over to a man in a uniform and asked, "Will there be another show later today?" The ranger said, "I'm afraid not. In fact, that was the last wrestling match of the season."

Disappointed, Paul quipped to Betty, "I guess the alligator won."

The Everglades National Park was in the area and, having been established just a few years prior, was one of the places they had heard about and wanted to visit. It was Betty's first time to see mangroves, marshes that seemed endless and beautiful white cranes. Her first view of real live palm trees was along the highway on their way south.

One day at the beach, Paul said it reminded him of one of the good memories from Korea, the day when the sergeant surprised them and took them to the shore. "That was a fun day. I didn't think Aunt Tonie would approve of me bringing my mattress along to the beach, though. Besides, I doubt it will float."

Betty smiled when she remembered watching the film of the day. "That was one of my favorite parts in the movies you sent. I kept running it back to see you splashing around and trying to catch a wave. It did my soul good to see you having such fun."

"Yeah, how'd you like those white boxers for swimming trunks?" Paul grinned.

Betty did not respond at first. "Well?" he insisted.

"You had to go and make me blush," she said finally, trying to hide her smile. "Okay, yes, like I said, it was one of my favorites. I was glad for your sake as well that you didn't have to swim in your fatigues!"

With just a couple days left of their vacation/honeymoon, they packed up and said thank you and farewell to their gracious hosts.

"I hope you enjoyed your stay and that we didn't interfere too much," Tonie said. "Sure hate to see you go. It's been a pleasure having you both and getting to know you a little better, Betty. Looks like the good Lord brought the two of you together and we wish you well. You come back anytime, you hear? You are always welcome."

"Now you two enjoy the Keys," said J.C. Then he added tongue-in-cheek, "And remember, you drive south to find them, before you head north for home."

Paul said, "Yep, got it Uncle J.C. Don't think I'll need my compass for this one. We'll look forward to seeing you in July at the family reunion. Thanks again for everything."

They drove toward the Florida Keys where they would spend their last night in Florida before they started the long drive home to Pennsylvania. They stopped at some shops and beaches before they crossed the famous Seven Mile Bridge.

Paul told Betty, "This bridge we're going to cross is the longest one in the country. It used to be a railroad bridge, until it was pretty much destroyed by a hurricane in '35."

Betty thought that sounded ominous. "Uh, hope it's safe now?"

"Oh yes, it's well traveled now! I read that the railroad couldn't afford to rebuild it, so the state bought it. They tore up the tracks and made it into a bridge for automobiles. Used to have to pay a toll, too, a whole dollar plus 25 cents per passenger. They just took away the tolls earlier this year, so we lucked out."

They neared the bridge and saw it looming ahead, stretching out like a pathway right into the sea.

Wide-eyed, Betty remarked, "It's unbelievable."

"It sure is a long bridge, but not as spectacular as the one in San Francisco," said Paul. "I've never been so glad to see a bridge in all my life! We sailed right under it and it was such a relief to know we were moments from setting foot on U.S. soil."

They reached their destination, a small boutique hotel where they would spend the night. They timed it just right to be able to check in, take their bags to their room and walk outside to watch the sunset complete with brilliant colors on display over the bay. They sat on a stone wall and Betty leaned back into Paul's strong arm around her.

She sighed with contentment. "What a perfect ending to a wonderful get-away with you."

Paul took in the moment, then said softly, "Thank you, Betty."

"For what dear?" she asked.

"Just for being you, beautiful you. You're so kind and gracious, fitting right in with my family and not minding where we stayed. And for waiting for me."

She sat straight up and looked at him. "Waiting for you? I made a vow to you, husband, that is forever. For better, for worse, for richer, for poorer, in sickness and in health, at home or in Korea. Of course I waited for you. Thank you for coming home to me. And for bringing me to Florida."

They looked into one another's eyes and Paul said, "I'm a better man being by your side. I'm so thankful God brought us together for this journey called life."

The seeds of love were planted at a sports banquet, kindled in a roller skating rink, consecrated by marriage, then complicated by war. That love had grown and now was reaffirmed by simple vows of recommitment, privately, together under God's watchful eyes.

The sun winked at them before it sank into the ocean in a splash of color. And God saw all that He had made and it was very good.

TWELVE

The story of Paul and Betty Nevel was not unlike many of the couples reunited after a period of military service. Betty continued her job as a secretary at the Metropolitan Life Insurance Company. Haller's Bakery hired Paul back on to deliver bread again. Habits from a year in the Army served him well; rise early, get to work on time and do the best possible job.

John Haller had come to Pennsylvania as an immigrant from Germany, and served an apprenticeship as a baker in Pittsburgh before moving to Altoona. After working at two established bakeries, he started his own. He and his family built a respected, successful business which thrived even through the Great Depression and was declared Pennsylvania's model bakery. Driving a bread truck was not what Paul wanted to do for the rest of his life, but he took pride in working for the reputable business and liked the interactions with customers. It was a job he was thankful to have. In Korea, he had endured far more difficult situations than a delivery route could throw at him and the memories were quite fresh.

After they got home from Florida, Mrs. Pope approached Paul after church one Sunday.

"I hope this question isn't out of place, but I was wondering if you and Betty will be looking for your own living space now that you're back from Korea. I know you gave up your first apartment when you had to leave."

"Yes, we'd like to get a little place of our own and have been saving towards that," Paul responded, "but haven't started looking yet."

Mrs. Pope smiled. "The reason I ask is that I might have just the place for you, an apartment on Sixth Avenue. It's small but just adorable, and I think it could be affordable for you."

"Well I certainly appreciate you thinking of us," a grateful Paul answered. "It would be nice to have you as a landlord."

Mrs. Pope was delighted to help. "Oh I'd be the lucky one to have you as tenants. Keep it in mind and make sure you talk to me when you are ready to look."

"Ok, I sure will," Paul replied. "I'll tell Betty about it and give you a call soon. Thank you so much, Mrs. Pope."

When the time seemed right, they talked to Mrs. Pope about renting her apartment. It was available, small but affordable and they were ready to have the privacy of a place of their own. Mrs. Pope lived next door and some of her family lived on the second floor. It was nice to know they would have good neighbors. Soon it was moving day. With some help from family and friends, they gathered the few things they had stored and began to set up house.

At the end of the day when all who had come to help were gone and most things were in place, Paul took Betty's hand and led her outside.

"Where are we going honey? We still have so much to organize…"

Paul answered, "I want to do this right, Mrs. Nevel."

Much to her surprise, he swiftly swept her off her feet and carried her across the threshold. She laughed as he sat her down on the couch and kissed her.

"This feels a bit like déjà vu," Paul said.

"I know. It's almost like having our first apartment was a false start and we get another chance. I can't wait to make this place our home. Promise me you won't leave me ever again."

"As much as it's up to me, and not the U.S. Army, I promise I am here to stay…as long as we both shall live."

They felt like they were starting out all over again as newlyweds.

One humid early August evening after a long, hot day at work, Paul was more than ready to get home and relax. Betty raced home from the insurance company and had been anxiously awaiting his arrival.

He gave her his usual greeting with a kiss. "Hi, honey, how was your day?" He could think of nothing better than a cool shower to rinse off a day of sweat and dirt. "What's for dinner?"

"It's a surprise," she responded with a twinkle in her eyes her clueless husband did not see, then twirled around and glided into the kitchen.

The couple was grateful for Mrs. Pope's apartment but dreamed of, and were saving for their own home. The economy of the middle to late 50s was one of optimism and expansion. A hardworking man could find a good job and decent pay. Prosperity and hope were hallmarks of America; tomorrow was going to be better than today.

Halfway to the bedroom, Paul sniffed the air and knew it was something that smelled delicious and the mystery intrigued him a bit. But first, that shower was calling him. By the time he came into the kitchen, the aroma was spectacular. Betty had his favorite meal of roast beef, mashed potatoes, fresh corn on the cob and her homemade sweet tea on the table.

"Well, my dear, this looks delicious," he remarked, still not seeing the unique expression on her face. "And you even got out the good dishes. What's the occasion?"

He took his place in anxious anticipation of a great evening to relax with his lovely wife, a delicious meal and a comfortable home. Life was good.

However, his wife sat down beside him and took his hand, not across the table where he could gaze at her and marvel how this woman chose to marry him…Wait, what…?

"Maybe it's just a thank you for working so hard to provide for us. I know days like today have to be tedious, in and out of the bread truck, working under the hot sun. I do love that tan on you, though!"

Paul grinned sheepishly. "So, just a thank you, huh? Well, my sweet wife, I am honored and it is very much appreciated. Thank you for the thank you."

They clasped hands and Paul gave God thanks, as was their custom before every meal. He dug in and filled his plate while Betty waited until Paul was in the middle of a scrumptious bite.

"Oh, and there is one other thing," she said softly.

"Hmm?" Which was man-speak for what is it and I have a mouth full of delicious food.

"You're going to be a daddy!"

The fork was poised to stab a chunk of meat when it fell onto the plate. He swiveled his head to see into her eyes, afraid to move the rest of his body.

"A daddy?"

She nodded with that gorgeous smile he loved so much, only this time it had a particular sparkle to it.

He jumped up and hugged her but then pushed her back to arm's length.

"I'm sorry!"

"Sorry?"

"I didn't mean to be so rough. Are you all right?"

"I'm pregnant, Paul, not injured," she laughed. "It's a perfectly natural thing to happen and I am fine with you holding me. In fact, hold me tighter."

And so he did. Then they kissed. They hugged some more but finally Betty decided they should eat. She had, after all, prepared his favorite meal and it should not be allowed to get cold.

Over the next few months the pregnancy progressed and regardless of her assurances to the contrary, Betty was not fine. Typical of what many women go through with such changes to their bodies, she had what doctors liked to call morning sickness. Yet her morning sickness happened to often last all day and sometimes made the need to go to work and even simple daily chores miserable.

Attempting to identify with her plight, Paul told her how her condition was much like his experience on the dreadful military ships.

To which she promptly replied, "Nice try, dear, but I don't think it's quite the same. In fact, I don't think there is any comparison."

"But have you ever been seasick?"

Turned out, that question was also a big mistake judging from the scowl and he quickly changed the subject, offering to get her crackers or milk or anything else that would allow him to relocate to another room.

By December when Betty continued to struggle with not just morning sickness, but all-day-sickness, they agreed that she should stop working at the insurance company. It was enough for her to take care of the house and to take care of herself and the little miracle growing inside her.

April approached and Paul found it harder to leave her to go to work on the bread truck. The closer they were to the due date, the more his mind taunted him. What if he missed the big event? What if he was not there when she needed him? What if, what if?

Then it finally happened. The contractions. Her water breaking. The panic and excitement on the way to the hospital. Watching his wife being wheeled away. The agonizing wait.

"It's a girl!" announced the nurse and Paul was allowed to go to Betty's room.

Somehow eight months of anticipation, preparation, work, play, and excitement mixed with a little worry had flown by for Paul but the nagging persistent nausea made it seem eternal for Betty.

When they first laid eyes on her and held their little bundle of joy on April 17th of 1956, they knew it was worth it all. She was born healthy and adorable and they named her Bonnie Lynn. With a full head of dark hair and sweet round cheeks, it was love at first sight for both of the proud parents. As the news traveled around to the grandparents and aunts and uncles, baby Bonnie had plenty of visitors, even though they could only see her through the glass of the nursery viewing window.

Mother and infant stayed in the hospital for five days, which was the average stay after a natural birth in those days. Betty was more than ready to go home.

When Paul carried Bonnie into the apartment for the first time, ready to celebrate, he suddenly crinkled up his nose and asked, "What is that smell?" He looked down at the sleeping baby, slightly concerned. "Is there something wrong?" he whispered.

No, it was just his first experience as a dad with a dirty diaper and Betty had to hide her amusement as he discovered the reality of parenthood.

Nevertheless, Paul was a quick learner and was not afraid to change a diaper or hold and soothe a crying baby. He seemed to be cut out for this father thing. His thoughts drifted back to the orphans in Korea; he knew he was going to do his best to be there and provide for this precious daughter God had entrusted to him.

That meant that a few changes had to take place.

Paul had many friends and family members who worked at the rail yards, and he heard that the Pennsylvania Railroad, known as PRR, was hiring. Though recently the hiring had surged and waned, it paid more than driving a delivery truck, so Paul took a chance and joined the ranks of many from Altoona in the past century by taking a job with the railroad. Unfortunately, the railroad was in decline from its heyday in the 1930s when Altoona reached its population peak as people from far and wide, including many immigrants from all over Europe, moved to Altoona to work for the famous railroad. The Altoona shops built tens of thousands of freight and passenger cars, maintained and repaired PRR's enormous fleet of engines and cars and turned out thousands of steam locomotives. In the 1950s, the more efficient diesel engines appeared on the scene, costing less to maintain and operate, gradually replacing the steam engine trains. In 1957, the last steam locomotive repair was completed in the Juniata shops of Altoona. Thus, Paul's job working for the railroad only lasted four months.

Ever since Paul was a little boy, he had a passion for building things. He excelled in his shop classes in high school and determined that he would be a carpenter one day. He and Betty wanted more children and his heart's desire was to be able to provide for his family so that his wife could be there for the kids every day. They decided together that she would not go back to full-time work, but when Bonnie was a few months old, could perhaps look for a part-time position.

When Paul was laid off from the railroad, he hoped it was his chance to find something where he could hone his skills and learn more about carpentry. He was hired by a small construction business, where he had the opportunity to pick up knowledge and skills about building and renovations on the job. But it was not guaranteed to be a long-term job.

Bob and Merilynn Hart were friends of the Nevels from church. A decade older than Paul and Betty, the couple became mentors and dear friends. They participated together in the church choir and other social activities and visited in one another's homes. Bob knew of Paul's search for work and told him about a contractor friend of his, Dan Horner. Yes, Paul had heard that he had built a reputable construction business in Altoona. Bob offered to introduce Paul and Dan, and Paul jumped at the opportunity.

Dan was initially impressed and thought Paul seemed like a fine young man. He especially liked his sincerity and enthusiasm for life. He believed such a man would be a hard worker so when he had an opening, he called Paul. It was just the opportunity a new father had been hoping and praying for. With thanksgiving to God on his lips, he went to work for Horner Construction and became an on-the-job apprentice, soaking up all he could about the literal "nuts and bolts" of construction.

Home construction was hard work and often called for long days, but he was determined to learn all he could and be the best carpenter possible. It was a thrill for Paul to be a part of careful measuring, hammering, sawing, and nail by nail, board by board, working with the other men to build a house from the ground up, creating it before their very eyes. The work was rewarding. There was also the mixture of outside and inside jobs, which was nice because the Pennsylvania climate offered every conceivable type of weather. Still, there were a few occasions when it was necessary to brave the not so pleasant conditions to put on a roof or side a house. But a man could feel good about what he accomplished at the end of a day.

Paul's sense of responsibility now heightened, and with their little apartment feeling smaller than ever, he thought it was time for them to implement their plan to have their own house built. Betty's monthly trips to the bank with her allotment of military pay was about to bring fruit. They had wisely saved their money and had enough for the 20% down payment required by banks in the 50s to finance a house. On quiet evenings or Sunday walks, they often talked about what kind of house they liked and could afford and what the rooms and layout would be. Paul sat down with his boss one day and told him they were ready. Horner's Construction was doing well and had been building homes in an area just outside of the downtown called Wehnwood. It was close to Ivyside Park, where Paul had learned to swim and ice skate. Dan agreed with Paul that it would be just the right place for them. Soon they began to build. The long days of hard physical labor somehow seemed less like work for Paul when he was seeing the dream of their very own house coming to fruition. His carpentry skills allowed them to save money by finishing the house on their own, now that he was confident in his own workmanship.

Betty often drove by the construction site on her way home from work to see the progress and to encourage Paul to please come home before dark and have some supper. The days were not as grueling for her but each day presented a set of challenges. She sent Paul off to work in the mornings with a good lunch packed in his metal lunch box, dressed and fed little Bonnie, then dressed herself and set out to accomplish her chores for the day. Sometimes her dad would bring her mother Betty to the apartment on his way to paint a house, to keep her company and play with Bonnie for the day.

One morning when Buck dropped off her mother, she came in, scooped up Bonnie, who was always excited to see Grandma, and smothered her with hugs and kisses, as usual. She then said to her daughter, "Honey, I wanted to let you know I heard they need a secretary at one of the other churches in town, Fifth Avenue United Methodist. Reverend Houser told me yesterday when I went to fix the flowers for the altar. They called to see if he could put the word out that they are looking. I told him I knew of an exceptional secretary who might be interested and he suggested that we call their church and said he would put in a good word for you."

"Oh Mom, that might be just the right thing for me. Did he say if it's part-time?"

"Yes, just two to three days a week. I would be happy to watch Bonnie for you, which would work out perfectly since the church is only a few blocks from our house."

"I am definitely interested. Shall I give him a call today? I'd be happy to apply and interview for the position."

Her mother said, "Sure, dear, give them a call. Reverend Houser agreed that it might be just the right fit for you. Oh, and I told him to make sure he tells the Fifth Avenue Reverend about how you were the fastest typist in your class and can take dictation with shorthand as quick as he can talk!"

Betty talked to Paul about it that evening and he agreed that it sounded like a great opportunity.

He paused as if in deep thought then said, "Amazing how God provides, at just the right time." The extra income would be needed when they moved in and set up house in Wehnwood.

Betty applied for, was offered and accepted the job at the church.

All the sacrifices, the difficult days and late nights finally paid off. The Paul Nevel family moved into their new home.

THIRTEEN

The first months in the new house in Wehnwood were filled with joy and the small family experienced the hope that had spread across the country that life would keep getting better. Bonnie was keeping them hopping as she grew and became more mobile, and was quite entertaining.

Their social life expanded. After Paul returned home from Korea, he and Betty had decided they should attend the same church to be able to serve as a team and so as not to confuse the children when children came along.

Betty loved the people at the Second Avenue Evangelical United Brethren Church. It was where she attended while growing up, where she had grown in her faith, and where she and Paul were married, which gave the building a special place in her heart. It was difficult for her to tell her friends about her decision to leave and even harder for her to tell her dear mother. But she continued to keep in touch with her church friends and to visit it for special services and programs. In time, all would see it was the best decision for their family.

There were Sunday church services, church socials and Sunday afternoon family gatherings for dinner. Harry and Dale had rotated home and were discharged. The army buddies and army wife buddies maintained contact with letters, holiday cards and the occasional phone calls. Since that was not enough for men who had faced one of the greatest experiences of their young lives together, the two men and their wives either made the trek to Altoona or the Nevel family drove to Allentown or Philadelphia to visit them. The former GIs were almost always focused on the future and rarely talked to family and friends about the events of their military service that brought them together. It was as though those memories were too personal to be voiced in public conversations. Or maybe it was the character of the sons and daughters of the World War II generation who were not braggadocios but humble in what part they played in their country's history.

Also, Glenn was home and having his best friend and constant source of amusement back in town was a delight for Paul. Glenn started talking about a girl he had met named Peggy. Paul questioned him, "When are we going to meet this new flame of yours?"

"Soon enough, brother Paul, soon enough."

The two had grown up together as first cousins and still laughed about a memory of Glenn's mother Ruba, who was Murry Nevel's sister and one of the Rudasill fifteen, known to the kids as Aunt Ruby. She had a parent/teacher conference with Glenn's teacher when he and Paul were in the same first grade class. The teacher said the only thing little Glenn had been vocal about was that he wanted to sit beside his brother, Paul. So apparently he had claimed Paul as his brother from an early age.

Glenn continued. "I've been testing the waters first. You know, not wanting her to be scared off when she meets the people I hang around with."

Paul smiled and said, "Understandable, but you're welcome to bring her to the house for a visit anytime. We will try not to embarrass you. Of course I can't make any promises."

Not long after that conversation, Glenn arranged with Paul to bring Peggy to meet him and Betty. The doorbell rang and Betty opened the door. Both Betty and Peggy just stared at each other for a brief moment, realizing this wasn't the first time they'd met.

Glenn was a little nervous. "Peggy, this is Betty, Betty, this is my girlfriend Peggy."

The ladies shook hands and Betty said, "Peggy! Nice to see you again."

Unbeknownst to Glenn or Paul, Betty had dated Peggy's brother in high school and he had brought Betty to their house a few times. It was an awkward moment, but it quickly passed as they explained their previous meeting to the guys and had a laugh about it.

"Glenn, when you started talking about this new friend named Peggy, I had no idea it was the same Peggy I knew," said Betty.

Paul felt a little jealousy rise up, even though he knew she had dated before but then, he reasoned, clearly she had chosen him. "Sorry about your brother's bad luck," joked Paul. "But not sorry she's all mine."

Betty blushed and Paul kissed her, then welcomed the couple inside. Bonnie had just started walking, so she provided the entertainment, waddling around with her hands up for balance. After Betty put her little one to bed, they sat around the kitchen table, talking and laughing over cups of hot tea and homemade chocolate chip cookies.

When summer was winding down, the unfortunate fragility of life intruded on their peaceful world. Paul received the call from Jake and rushed over to the hospital. Murry Nevel had suffered from multiple strokes off and on over the previous couple of years. This time a massive stroke took her life. She passed on to join James in September of 1957. The shock of losing both parents when they were only in their forties bore down on Paul as he realized he and his siblings were orphans. The weight of being the oldest child meant many decisions concerning his mother's funeral and personal affairs fell to him. Once again, his rock, comfort and solace was Betty. Their partnership was tested by the trials of life and always grew stronger because of them. Around them were also a church family and a community to draw upon for support.

Having a larger house sure came in handy and they were thankful for it. Paul's youngest brother was still in high school and Paul considered Tom to be his responsibility. So, his sibling moved into the guest room in the new house. When Tom finished high school that next spring, his dream was to follow in his big brother's footsteps and serve his country. He was interested in mechanics and airplanes, so he planned to join his chosen branch of the service, the Air Force. Paul was his hero and though Paul was proud of him, he was naturally concerned and prayed for peacetime to continue around the world.

That fall, there was a joyous occasion as well. Paul and Betty spent a lot of time with Glenn and Peggy, going to church together and various outings and events. Paul told Betty he knew his cousin well enough to know that there was something different about how Glenn felt for this girl. He was right. Glenn popped the question to Peggy. It was Paul's turn to take on the honors of best man. To Glenn's chagrin, Paul promised that he would be just as good of a best man as Glenn had been. Yes, indeed, he would be right there to catch his cousin if he fell or tried to run away. Needless to say, Glenn knew he deserved the retaliation. He reminded Paul that he also had met his wife at the roller skating rink so Paul was not the only roller skating Casanova in Altoona.

Glenn and Peggy became Mr. And Mrs. Glenn Ardrey on October 19, 1957. They moved into Paul and Betty's old apartment with Mrs. Pope for a landlord.

One cold December evening in 1958, Paul arrived home frozen from a day on the construction site and was hit in the face with a pleasant aroma when he entered the house. His nose told him it was Betty making his favorite dinner; what a treat after a long and frigid day. He stopped. The table was set with their good dishes and his mind swirled. Had he forgotten something; a special day? Betty's birthday was a month prior. His was not until February.

While Betty hummed and put the food on the table, he fetched little Bonnie and put her in her highchair, all the time fretting about what he might have forgotten and why he could not remember whatever it was that he forgot. They prayed and he considered adding a note to God about forgiveness as a reminder to his wife that God is forgiving and she should be as well.

"You know, this is all wonderful, honey," he remarked casually as they passed the dishes. "You haven't put out the good dishes for no reason since…" Of course, he could not remember when the last time was but he was hoping for a hint.

"The last time I told you that I was pregnant?" Betty suggested coyly.

"Yeah," Paul beamed. Sure, he remembered that night when…

He looked at Betty. He looked at Betty's tummy. He looked at Betty and beamed.

"Pregnant?"

The second pregnancy was not any easier for Betty. She hoped and prayed the sickness would not last as long, but unfortunately, Betty was destined to once again endure nearly nine months of nausea. She continued her job at the church, and her boss, the Reverend, was understanding and gave her flexibility to be able to come and go according to how she felt. On the good days, she tried to work ahead so that it would make up for the bad days. Another drawback was that she was the most pregnant during the hottest part of the year. There were not enough fans to keep her cool.

On the 21st of August, 1958, after being on a construction site all day,

Paul was cleaning a business building the Horner crew had built just blocks from their new house when a neighbor came running up to tell him to get home quick. The baby was on its way.

Gail Elaine Nevel arrived later that evening. With a lighter complexion and thin blonde hair, she did not look much like her sister, but little Bonnie was sure she was her twin. She took her role of big sister very seriously, even at two years old, and was a big help to mommy.

Paul worked hard at his job to provide and did his share of the chores around the house. Dwight D. Eisenhower was in his second year as President of the United States of America and the country was at relative peace having settled into the idea that the world was divided into the free West and the communist East. The American spirit of the times was that there were no obstacles which could not be overcome and no dream too big to dream. It should be no surprise, then, that Paul had a dream, one buried in the back of his mind. And every once in a while, he would take it out and think about it, but then life would intervene and he would put it away, again.

But Paul Nevel had endured the horrors of long sea voyages while suffering from seasickness, faced the prospects of going to war, served his country living and working under harsh conditions in a foreign land and had dared to hold hands with the most beautiful woman in Altoona while skating to the Blue Danube under soft lights. He could dream big dreams and expect that they might come true.

FOURTEEN

Marlene Myers had gone away to study at a Methodist affiliated college in central Pennsylvania, Lebanon Valley College. She started writing home about a nice handsome young man she met named Marvin Rice. He was studying to be a Methodist minister.

> *Dear Betty, I think I've found the man of my dreams. He's not tall, dark and handsome, but rather is tall, redheaded and handsome. He's so kind-hearted and makes me laugh. I never thought I would want to be a preacher's wife, but I'm starting to change my mind about that. I can't wait for you to meet him and for him to meet you.*

Betty remembered when the two sisters would sit up at night in whispered conversations about boys and love. She knew love now and her sister's letters reminded her so much of how she felt about Paul. She could not be happier for Marlene.

It was not long before Marlene and Marvin were on their way to Altoona so he could meet her family. Poor Marvin had the look of a deer in the headlights with Buck grilling him on his life story and future plans, and Mother Betty filling him with pie. Apparently, he was a brave soul because he still asked Buck for his daughter's hand in marriage. He proposed to Marlene soon after and she accepted.

Their beautiful wedding was the social event of the Myers and Nevel family for that year. It was held at the Second Avenue Evangelical United Brethren Church where Betty and Marlene had grown into young ladies and Paul and Betty were married. Marlene asked Betty to be her maid of honor, but it was when big sister was very pregnant with baby number two. Betty decided she would not look good in a bridesmaid gown, so she passed along the honor to Marlene's best friend. Little Bonnie was dressed and ready to be the flower girl, except when the day came, at the last minute, the two-year-old was too shy to walk down the aisle in front of all those people. She sure liked her fancy dress, though, and showed it off to everyone at the reception.

The mother of the bride thought her husband Buck looked just as handsome walking their second daughter proudly down the aisle as he did with the first one. She would have to check his fingernails for paint, though. Why did she always think of it when it was too late? Tall, handsome Marvin was beaming as he watched his bride, looking every bit like the future pastor.

After his graduation, Marvin took a ministerial position at a church in Greencastle, Pennsylvania. Betty missed her sister terribly and the three-hour drive from Altoona meant they seldom saw each other. They wrote letters to keep in touch. Marlene and Marvin had their first baby, Mark, in August of '61 and their second, Marcia, soon after in November of '62. When they were able to visit each other, the kids were adorable playing together and got along quite well with one another.

One November evening, Betty set up yet another special dinner for Paul to announce that number three was on his or her way. She thought surely he had caught on by now, though she threw him some curve balls from time to time. Men, what happened to their ability to read minds? Anyway, since five years had passed from the last time, he had an excuse if the announced pregnancy took him a little by surprise. Bonnie and Gail were in on the announcement this time, so they made it quite the joyful occasion, excitedly clapping and screaming and dancing around the living room after supper.

Lord, have pity on the child who came third into a family. The newness of the excitement and anticipation had worn off a bit. There were fewer photos taken of the pregnant mother who was wearing clothes several years out of style and had too much going on to pose. The life of child number three would be one of hand-me-downs and leftovers from the previous two siblings, used toys, a used crib and used cloth diapers.

Daughter number three, Julie Sue, was born in July of 1963. Bonnie was seven years old and Gail was soon to be five. The girls were more than thrilled to welcome another sister! She was their very own living doll baby to play with, complete with smiles and dimples. Ah yes, little Julie had drawers and closets full of clothes to wear for years to come.

With his growing family, Paul began to think more seriously about a move to the country and would go to look at land from time to time. His dream came out of hiding and he talked about it with his brothers and sister, with Glenn and his other friends, and especially with Uncle Ken. Betty maintained her reservations, especially about leaving their home that he helped to build, but she tried to be fair and continued to listen. Besides, she maintained that it was still years away, if it ever did become a reality.

FIFTEEN

One evening in late autumn of 1964, Paul picked up the mail before he came in the house after work.

"Honey, you have a letter from your sister."

Betty rushed from the kitchen. "Oh wonderful, let me see."

She was always happy to hear from Marlene and to get the latest news. A letter from her sister was a nice change from the daily routine. She tore open the envelope and sat down on her rocking chair in the living room to read her letter, scooping up Julie to sit on her lap. The first words made her blood run cold.

"Oh no, no, no, no…!" Paul was leafing through the other mail, a bill and some advertisements. He saw the alarm on her face. "What's wrong?"

"She's been to the doctor."

Betty began to read aloud.

A mole on my shoulder had been bothering me as it was itchy and seemed to have gotten bigger and changed colors. The first doctor I went to wasn't alarmed and just burned it off. It didn't heal very well and I wasn't feeling good, so we went to another doctor. He didn't like the looks of it and took a biopsy.

She could barely speak the next few words.

Betty, the biopsy came back positive for melanoma. It's a form of skin cancer. The doctor said they'll have to do more tests to see if it has spread. But he said it's treatable, so I'm waiting to hear what's next. Please pray for me and pray for Marvin. The kids are too young to understand of course, but they sense Mommy has been a bit stressed

and tired. I haven't told Mom and Dad yet. I hate to worry any of you.
But I thought maybe you could go over to the house and have them
call me when you're there with them. Marvin is being so supportive,
and we know this is in God's hands.

Hearing the word cancer is always a scary thing. Modern medicine has made a diagnosis of cancer a little less frightening. Yet in the early 60s, it was a terrifying word to say to someone. Betty could only think the worst for her sister.

"Paul, I'm scared for her. Oh I pray it's not too serious. I'll go to Mom's tomorrow after work and we can call Marlene when Dad gets home."

Naturally, Betty did not sleep well that night and could not shake the feeling of dread about what her sister might be facing.

The next day, she took the girls over to see Gram and Pap Pap and they made the call. She had known sorrow from the tragedies in Paul's family, now it had come to those she loved the most. Though she put the best possible spin on the news that she could, none of the Myers family would have a good night's sleep for some time to come.

A couple of weeks went by and the test results came back positive for cancer in Marlene's lymph nodes. It had already spread. If only the first doctor had been proactive and cut out the mole, the diagnosis might have been different. It was a difficult Christmas that year, as the family tried to remain positive especially for the children's sake, but they saw Marlene declining and getting weaker by the day. She had to give up playing piano at the church and Marvin hired a nanny to help with the children.

By the beginning of February, it was decided that Marlene should be hospitalized.

Marvin took her to Philadelphia to the University of Pennsylvania Hospital where the best doctors in the state practiced. He later called his in-laws and said things did not look good and they should probably come if they wanted to see her.

"Buck, I'm so afraid and she must be terrified," said Betty after the call. "She needs her mom; we just need to go."

Buck did not hesitate, "I'll let the guys know we won't be painting tomorrow. Pack a bag for us both and let's get on the road."

It was a harrowing, agonizing six-hour drive from Altoona for Buck and Betty and they could not reach Philadelphia fast enough. They went from winding roads in the country to three lane highways with terrible traffic. When driving through Philadelphia, Buck was glad the hospital had at least given him good directions. They parked in the hospital parking garage and made their way to the main entrance to ask the receptionist for information.

The receptionist checked the location. "ICU, Room 2665 for Marlene Rice. You'll go down the hall and take a right to get to the elevators."

They hurried to the elevators, went in and pushed the button for the second floor. The jolt of the elevator moving made Betty's stomach queasier than it already was. The doors opened and they followed the room number signs. At last they saw her room number on a door and walked into the room.

"It's empty. No one's here. Buck, they must've given us the wrong room number. Didn't they say 2665? I don't see Marvin anywhere."

"I thought so, but let's ask at the nurse's station. Must be a different room," said Buck. He was trying to be strong but his mind could only think of the absolute worst. "Hope we're at least on the right floor."

They went to the desk to ask, "We are Marlene Rice's parents. We got the wrong room information for our daughter. Which room is she in?"

The nurses behind the desk looked at one another. One said, "Um, Marlene was on our floor, but they just took her…"

"Oh, okay good, I knew we just had the wrong information. Where will we find her?" asked a hopeful Buck.

"Sir, ma'am, I'm so very sorry to have to tell you this, but she has passed on. We did all we could."

Passed on? Passed on! The shock of the news sent Buck and Betty reeling. What did that nurse just say? She's gone? Our daughter is gone? Why? No, this isn't real, this can't be happening! Why couldn't we have gotten here in time to see her? Did she know we were coming? Why had God allowed this? Why now, why her? She was only 29 years old. With two young children. Oh the little ones…poor, poor babies, let us see the children, we need to hold the children.

While the two parents were dealing with their pain, Marvin managed to find them. There had been formalities to deal with, even for a grieving husband; papers to sign, instructions given. They hugged, they cried, they mourned.

Marvin experienced the hardest part of the heartbreaking episode, telling Mark and Marcia that Mommy would not be coming home. How grateful he was to have these two amazing little human beings that he and Marlene had brought into the world. He thanked God for them, but at the same time, grieved that their little hearts had to go through this pain. They would be sad and miss her for a long time to come.

Paul and Betty reached out to Marvin as much as they could in the midst of their own sorrow. Paul tried to imagine how Marvin must have felt and could not even conceive in his mind how he would survive if he lost his darling wife. Betty was heartbroken. She had lost her only sister and best friend. It did not seem to make much sense at all.

"Paul, it's so hard to understand," she said one long night as they lay in bed, unable to sleep. "I know we need to trust God. I didn't want her to suffer and now she's in heaven and much better off than we are down here. But I'm going to miss her so."

The funeral at Marvin's church in Greencastle was a beautiful tribute to a beautiful life. People came from everywhere to pay their respects, as Marlene had many friends and everyone who knew her thought so much of her. The parishioners reached out to try and comfort their young pastor and his children. Lots of tears were shed for a young woman whose life was cut far too short.

In the Myers family, Buck and Betty suffered the most. No parent should ever have to bury their child and regardless of the age, it is never an easy thing to do. Through the tears, all that Buck could say was, "My queen Marlene, my sweet, sweet Marlene."

After the service, the women from the church served a meal for those in the family. Then everyone went back to Marvin's house. That night, no one wanted to leave, as if to do so would be to forget her. Eventually, the family left Marvin and the two kids but only after he promised to visit as often as possible.

Paul shook Marvin's hand, then quickly thought better of it and hugged him. "You come visit us now, you hear?" Paul said. "The kids will have a ball together. We'll always be family and are just a phone call away."

The drive back to Altoona was long and quiet.

SIXTEEN

Throughout their first thirteen years of marriage, Paul and Betty had realized some of their dreams and often talked about those early days of courtship and marriage. They felt even stronger as a couple after they had withstood the test of being separated by Paul's mandatory service in the Army, the deaths of both of Paul's parents, Marlene's passing and the other ups and downs of life in general. They were blessed with a nice house, good employment and three beautiful baby girls for which they thanked God every day. Betty loved where they lived. She thought they had wonderful neighbors and they were just across town from her parents. Paul liked it, too, but could not deny a stirring deep within him, a dream he brought up to Betty from time to time in their quiet moments. She would nod and maybe make a comment, then he would send it back to its safe place for a while.

The neighborhood in which they lived had grown and they were just another part of suburbia. Paul never intended for that to go on forever. He longed for wide open space and for much more than their half acre with a tiny garden. Lord willing, not to mention Betty willing, he would achieve his dream.

What might be called the path to Asbury Lane began as the seed of the dream started to grow little by little. After a bedtime snack, teeth-brushing and prayers, the girls had just been put down for the night and Betty dropped into her favorite chair to savor a cup of tea. Paul was dwelling on his dream and had been thinking about it all day while mostly going through the motions on the construction site.

"Someday," he said softly, "I still want to buy a farm, you know."

"Yes, I know," she said, her eyes closed; it was peaceful and serene.

"The farm next to Uncle Ken's is for sale."

A warning bell went off in Betty's mind. Uncle Ken's farm was over an hour away from where they lived. She had hoped and prayed if and when the day came when they moved, it would at least be close to Altoona.

"But Paul, that's so far away. Are you really sure that you want to be a farmer?" she asked, ever so carefully.

"I'm sure, Betty. I loved my summers working on Uncle Ken's farm, from the time I was old enough to be around the equipment until I graduated from high school." Betty saw the glint in his eyes and heard the passion in his voice, which was nothing new when he talked about this dream of his. "I'm just so intrigued by the entire process of preparing the land, sowing seeds, watching them grow and then bringing in the harvest. I'd love to have a huge garden, especially with lots of corn. And horses – I'm fond of horses, you know." He loved horses and had been around cows, some goats and ducks. His uncle showed him by example how to treat both large and small animals, and to properly care for them.

"I guess I don't know much about farm life, other than the things you've talked about." Betty conceded. "I haven't been around many animals, other than a few house cats, but I don't think I want the hassle of having pets in the house."

"Okay, but we will need some outside cats, you know, barn cats, to chase the mice away..."

"Eek! Mice? Do there have to be mice?" she asked, a little panicked.

"Sure, every good barn has some mice in it." He chuckled. "Don't worry, my dear, we'll do our best to keep them out of the house and in the barn."

Betty humored him when the subject of a farm came up, but she figured it would still be several years until they could afford to buy a farm. Maybe he would change his mind by then. Or maybe she would be ready to give being a farmer's wife a try.

"It's a lot of hard work, you know," she said. "And I know you're a hard worker, but how will you keep up with taking care of land and animals, plus working another full time job? And then there's the little matter of me and the girls. Will we ever see you?"

"When the time is right, I'll manage. You'll see. We'll manage together, and it'll be worth it."

Paul believed he knew what it took and that he would step up to the task. He had watched his uncle fluctuate between frustration and patience when they had to wait out inclement weather to bring the hay in or when they needed more rain for the crops. Uncle Ken had bad days when he had to deal with broken equipment or the cows ran through the fence again. But now was not the time to mention those things. He realized the life of a farmer included early mornings and late nights and a lot of hard work in between. But there was something about it that attracted him; the sweat on his brow, the rewards of his labor, biting into a fresh ripe juicy tomato for which he had planted the seed himself. There was nothing better after a hard summer day's work than sitting down to one of his aunt's delicious suppers of homegrown food and the banter around the table between the family and farm hands about the day's activities. Someday, he hoped and dreamed, he would be the farmer sitting down to Betty's meal of fresh homegrown food.

SEVENTEEN

The world outside of Altoona was confusing with the assassination of President John F. Kennedy and military escalation in some corner of the world known as Vietnam. The Nevels mourned with the country and wondered what was happening to the moral fiber of the nation. Lyndon B. Johnson was successor to the presidency and though Americans were unsure about their armed forces being involved in yet another foreign war, at least Johnson was coming from war experience as he had seen action in World War II and was a decorated U.S. Naval Reserve Veteran. For Paul and Betty's generation, the beginning of the conflict in Vietnam had similarities to Korea. Nevertheless, the thought was not a pleasant one that other couples, other families might have to put their lives on hold and sacrifice one or two years because of military obligations. They had a perspective that those in Washington might not have.

Paul and Betty continued to work, save money and raise their daughters in their friendly neighborhood. They enjoyed entertaining friends and family and the girls had an abundance of playmates between their cousins, neighbors and church friends. Betty continued to work as a secretary at Fifth Avenue United Methodist Church, as they were flexible with her schedule and allowed her to work between having the babies. It provided extra income to boost their savings or when Paul's work was slow due to weather. Gram, as Betty's mother was called by the three girls, loved the opportunities to babysit. As for Betty, she was unaware that she was ahead of her time; a wife and mother working outside the home. In the 60s era before prepackaged foods, domestic cleaning services, takeout restaurant food and automatic household appliances, most women left the workforce when they married because of the full-time daily demands of keeping a house and raising children.

Paul preferred to listen to the radio even after television became more popular. He especially liked talk radio; one program in particular was his favorite, Paul Harvey's News and Comment. The opinions Harvey expressed were old-fashioned and to Paul's liking. Politically and socially conservative, the radio personality also believed in the American dream.

The years passed with the family falling into the routines of life: home, work, school, church. Each season brought its own set of activities, joys, and challenges. Then Betty began to feel a little nauseated in the mornings. At first, she thought she had a bug and tried to push through it. Unfortunately, the sickness persisted. With her sister very much on her mind, she wisely decided a visit to the doctor was warranted. Needless to say, she left the doctor's office surprised.

The growing little girls were the focus of the Nevels' lives and three seemed a perfect number of children for their family. Yet, once again God had other plans for Paul and Betty and, this time, she was the one surprised by her condition. Driving home, she worried about how her husband might react. She knew he would also be worried about how they were going to feed and provide for yet another baby. While she considered how she would tell him and mentally composed the menu for that special meal she would prepare, he guessed that she was growing a new little life. The morning sickness was back again and he noticed.

This time, though, he did not make the mistake of telling her how much he understood her nausea. He remembered that a pregnant woman does not like to have her condition compared to seasickness. Yep, this pregnancy he just told her how sorry he was for her suffering and fetched the crackers and water and anything else she needed. Who said that men cannot learn from their mistakes?

"I don't know how this happened," she remarked, after Paul told her what he had suspected when the girls were safely tucked away for the night.

"I do," he volunteered.

"Not funny, Paul." At that moment, Betty did not really appreciate her husband impersonating Glenn's sense of humor.

"Honey, you know we are running out of space here and I would really like to find a farm and have our family there before this baby is born," Paul reasoned with his wife. "I know you like living where we are and I will miss this house too. But I will build you another home."

Betty looked around. Another home? How could any other house replace this home where her family had enjoyed so many great moments and endured some of the pains of life? Then there were her flowers outside and the garden; how could she leave them? The saplings they planted when they first moved in were now trees.

However, she was realizing that the house she loved that had seemed so big the day they moved in was suddenly quite small and shrinking.

"It will be an adventure," continued Paul. "I promise you, if you will agree to move to where we have some land and room to grow, I will build you a new house."

All Betty was capable of doing was to nod and tearfully lean into his embrace. She knew he always kept his promises. Silently she prayed that it would be somewhere not too far away, a place that would be just right for them and would even be the answer to Paul's dream.

"I guess I have trusted you too long to not trust you, now, oh Lord," she prayed in her heart.

Her resistance finally melting into peace, she managed to say, "Okay, Paul, I think I'm ready. Besides, you know I'll follow you anywhere."

As a couple, they had come a long way from that Saturday when she opened the pink plastic egg and discovered the perfect engagement ring. She had trusted in his love when he was far away in Japan, California and finally Korea. Her trust in him carried them through three pregnancies and a few family traumas. Her husband had always sacrificed for his wife and children. She could only believe that he would do what was best for her and their family, even if that was not what she wanted to do. God had blessed her with a great man; it was time to continue trusting him and trusting God.

Though Paul and Betty hoped together for a son from the unexpected pregnancy, Paul heard that now familiar exclamation from the doctor bursting into the waiting room with, "It's a girl!" Daughter number four was born in July of 1966, sixteen days after Julie Sue's third birthday. Julie thought the new baby was her very own belated birthday present. With an adorable head of dark hair and big brown eyes, Karen Jane arrived with great celebration by her older sisters and was welcomed into the family.

Meanwhile, a farm and new house large enough to accommodate the growing family was yet to be located, but it would not be long.

One warm September day when she was in the bedroom folding a mountain of clothes she had taken off of the clothes line, Betty heard the phone ring. She knew Paul had answered it, but could not hear what the conversation was about. Anyway, her mind was on the dozens of chores she had to do and a few her husband needed to put on his list.

She walked into the living room to hear him say, "Thanks a million, Jim. It sounds like what we've been looking for. I'm going to call right now and ask if I can go see it. I'll let you know and would love for you to go along. Thanks again."

Paul hung up the phone and turned to look at Betty with a wide smile on his face and a giddy tone to his voice. "Honey, Jim Harding called about a farm he has made deliveries to on his route for Diamond Supply. He was unloading bottled gas there the other day and the owner talked about possibly selling before too long. Tonight he saw it listed in the classifieds in the Mirror. A dairy farm for sale, 110 acres."

"A…dairy farm?" she responded.

But he was not listening. He had the paper in his hand and was leafing through looking for the ad. "Jim knows right where it is and offered to go with me to look at it."

"Paul, a dairy farm? You mean a place where they milk cows?"

"It's only about five miles from here."

"But I…," Betty stopped. "Five miles?"

Paul shook his head and showed her the ad in the Altoona Mirror.

"Yes, call them, hurry!" she exclaimed. "Call now!"

Five miles was practically like being next door, at least compared to the other prospects he had come across near Uncle Paul or in another county.

Immediately, Paul pulled out the thick Altoona area phone book from a drawer and began to leaf through the yellow pages for the number of a realtor he knew. His dad was a barber and when he cut Paul's hair, he often gave updates on his son's success with selling houses and land. Paul called him and made an appointment for the next day. He called Jim back and they agreed to meet up and go see the property. Jim's wife Judy wanted to join them. Then Paul rushed out.

All the while, Betty stood there wondering what she should do.

Suddenly, Paul hurried back into the house, took her in his arms and kissed her before he ran out again.

She savored the moment. Then one of the girls cried and a new crisis called her.

After Paul visited the farm with Jim and Judy, he took Glenn to see it. He valued his cousin's advice. When Glenn saw the cows lining up right behind the house they would live in and the house's condition, he was not too keen on the idea.

"I don't know, Paul," he said, trying not to crush his cousin's enthusiasm. "Betty might not go for this. That little house needs a lot of work. And those cows will keep you up at night."

In his mind, Paul saw something different.

"That is just where we will live temporarily." They walked on and Paul explained the vision he had for the property. "I can build a better house. I can picture it, right there on the hill. Oh and they're taking the cows with them."

"Well, that's good then," said Glenn, a glint in his eye. "But how will they mooove them?" He laughed at his own joke then added slyly, "I hope they leave a few of the barn cats to chase away the mice."

"Oh, believe me, I've already told Betty we will have cats to keep the mice at bay."

The first time Paul took Betty to see the farm, she noticed the road sign as they turned by the little red brick Methodist church on the corner. She read it out loud, "Asbury Lane, hmmmm…" She said it again, "Asbury Lane."

It had a nice ring to it, a charming quality.

Just as they turned onto the lane, there was a long, steep hill with a few houses on each side. At the top of the hill, the road curved to the right and over another little knob, then down and around. The dirt road seemed to have been well kept. They took another few turns on the winding road and then went straightway onto the farm. The tree-lined lane took a gradual straight climb, another bend, up another bit of a hill and there stood the big red barn looming before them. The stark red against the green trees that were just beginning to turn to orange, red and yellow in their fall colors seemed to offer a friendly welcome. Turning left at the bend in the road by the barn led to two houses at the end of the lane.

The house on the left was the original farmhouse that the Kutruffs who were selling the farm intended to keep. The one on the right was the little rustic house that would be where the Nevels would live.

"I know it's small, Betty, but we'll make the most of it until I can build the house I promised you," said Paul as he pulled the car up to it.

When they walked in, Betty's heart sank as it hardly compared to their newer, nicer, more spacious house in Wehnwood. The front door led into the kitchen where there was an old metal sink and two metal cupboards. Next was the living room area, then two steps led down to a bedroom on the right and a bedroom on the left. Through the bedroom on the left was another room that had been added on. The house had been built in three different sections, so it was an unusual layout. At one time it had been a springhouse, where water ran off the mountain and came into the cold cement block basement to be collected for use. The upper level of the house was used to store large cans of milk from the cows the Kutruffs owned.

Mr. Kutruff worked for the railroad and they sold what was called jug milk to individuals as a business on the side.

While all Betty could see was the extent to which they would be digressing from their present residence, Paul was seeing into the future and could envision so much more than her mind could grasp.

They walked through the rooms and talked about who and what would go where. Her dad Buck had already offered to paint the rooms whatever color Betty wanted. It was little consolation to what she was seeing.

But then they walked outside and Paul pointed out possibilities for where the new house would be built and the wide-open spaces just waiting for some special little girls looking for adventure and she began to put it together in her mind and catch his dream. She felt some relief knowing the kids would have lots of room to roam and how they would love it here…outside the house at least. Besides, she reminded herself, it is love that makes a home and they had plenty of that to go around.

The days flew by once the property was purchased. Paul's brother, Tom, who was still serving in the United States Air Force, pitched in from his savings to help them make the down payment. The farm had an R.D. address number, meaning rural delivery. They were truly in the country.

Paul and Buck spent many hours working to fix up the old house. Paul tended to what needed repaired in each room while his father-in-law came after him and painted the walls and ceilings. While the men worked on getting the little house into shape, Betty was busy at home trying to take care of four children while packing up their belongings. She was glad for her mom's assistance and also counted on Bonnie and Gail, now 10 and 8 years old, to help out with little 3-year-old Julie and 3-month-old Karen.

Bonnie and Gail were unhappy at first with the prospects of leaving their neighborhood friends and changing schools. Paul told them, "But just wait 'til you see the farm. You will love it." When they walked around the little house as their mom showed them where their new rooms would be, Bonnie noticed her mother wiping her eyes and blowing her nose. Betty passed it off as catching a cold or allergies, but Bonnie sensed her sadness. Her 10-year old mind went right to protecting her mom.

"It'll be okay, Mom. We'll have fun bringing our things here and figuring out where everything goes. Dad said he'll go with us to our first day of school. And he said we're getting horses."

Gail chimed in, "Yay, horses! We wouldn't have room for horses in Wehnwood, would we Mom?"

It did help ease the lump in Betty's throat when she saw their excitement.

Ernie and Ruth Wissinger were friends Paul and Betty knew from church. They owned several grocery stores in the area and Ernie had built a respected reputation as an honest, well-liked and successful businessman in the community. They owned a few acres of land and would host church picnics and pool parties at their place. They had two horses purchased for their children to ride, but now their children were off to college. When Ernie heard Paul was buying a farm, he approached him with a proposition. He did not have a good place to winter the horses and offered to give his two horses to Paul if he would feed them over the winter, and they could discuss whether or not he would keep them in the spring. Paul was pleased with the idea. It fit perfectly into his dream for the pasture land and use of the barn. The problem was how to get the animals all the way across town to the farm, as he had no access to a horse trailer.

Paul had an idea. Melvin was Paul's cousin, several years younger, liked horses and was always up for an adventure. Paul gave him a call.

"Hey Mel, how would you like to go for a horseback ride?"

Without hesitating or asking why or what that meant, Melvin said, "Sure. When and where?" He was always excited to saddle up.

Glenn drove Paul and Melvin to the Wissinger farm where they saddled the horses and were off like John Wayne riding the trail in his latest western epic. However, Glenn thought they looked more like Andy Devine, the sidekick to many a Western hero.

The ride ended up being longer and more of an adventure than they expected as Melvin later told Paul he could not sit down in school for the next three days.

The day after the horses took up residence on the farm, it was moving day for the Nevel family.

❧

And so it was on Betty's 34th birthday, November 10, 1966, Paul and Betty and their four daughters moved to a farm at the end of Asbury Lane.

Those early days on the farm were busy for the family while they adjusted to a smaller house and being outside of town. Friends came to visit and see this farm they'd heard about. Betty was always a gracious host as she tried to make this house a home, offering a meal, or at least a piece of her delicious chocolate cake.

The only neighbors close by were the Kutruffs, who had sold the farm to their son Bill initially because they were getting up in years, and Bill sold it to Paul. They kept an acre of land with the original farm house where they lived until their deaths. Paul, in turn, sold a few acres to their son Tom Kutruff and his wife Sevilla after Tom's parents passed some years later. With Paul's help, Tom built a house and a small barn down towards the beginning of the lane. Paul later sold one acre to his sister Myra Sue and also helped to build her house. His construction skills continued to prove to be a blessing to those he knew.

Bill Kutruff sold Paul a tractor that was an old hand crank red Farmall, a good name for reliability and considered one of the first all-purpose tractors on the market. It had replaced a team of horses among farmers as an efficient and cost-effective method of working a farm. Paul's brother Jake had acquired a genuine mechanic ability from tinkering on cars and assured his brother that he could help keep it running for a few more years.

Bonnie and Gail were nervous about attending their first day in a new school called Myers Elementary. Their new place of residence was just over the school district boundary line which put them into the Bellwood-Antis School District, rather than the larger Altoona schools. Paul and Betty heard great things about the small town of Bellwood and its schools and believed this to be a blessing. Paul kept his promise and drove them to school that day, knowing they had been through a lot of change lately and going to a new school could be traumatic. He walked in with them to check in at the office and made sure they found their classrooms. He was anxious for them and breathed a prayer as he drove away that they would soon be making friends and would adapt quickly.

EIGHTEEN

It was not paradise, but it would become the next best thing to it.

Moving in November gave them a little time to get somewhat settled before winter kicked in. The first winter on the farm gave new meaning to "Winter Wonderland," as the snow fell and blanketed the hills and landscape around them. As much as Betty hated the thought of driving in it, she had to admit it made for a beautiful winter farm scene.

The girls were more than excited to build snowmen and igloos and to try out the hills with their sleds and saucers. There were the beginnings of Sunday afternoon visits from friends and relatives which would become a regular part of the weekends on Asbury Lane. Paul tried to stay ahead of the snow and keep the lane plowed. If their cars could make it up the lane, their friends knew they would be in for a good time. Bundled up against the cold and sledding down the hills or the lane, they would then go inside for Betty's hot chocolate. Also, there were two ponds that Paul cleared off when he was sure they were frozen solid enough. He allowed the kids and adults to try their hand, or their feet, at ice skating.

Before long, Christmas would arrive and there was plenty to do to prepare for it. Paul was excited for them to have their very own woods from which they could cut their very own Christmas tree for this special first Christmas on the farm. Betty helped Bonnie and Gail bundle up to head out into the cold with their dad, and gave in to little Julie's pleas of "Me, too! I want to go!" So another one bundled, off they went, Paul and three excited girls, ax, saw, bailing twine and sled.

They returned a couple hours later with their chosen tree and frozen fingers. Betty prepared the hot chocolate as Paul drug the blue spruce through the door and into the living room. He held it up as they all stood around it.

Holding Karen in her arms, Betty glanced sideways at Paul as she stated what he was also thinking, "Uh, very nice, but... isn't it a little bare and lopsided?" Disappointment gave way to giggles as they all realized it looked very different in their living room than it had looked in the woods!

A trip to town later that day resulted in a better-looking tree for the living room and some extra lights for their still special treasured find, which would literally "spruce up" the small front porch of the little house. The girls hung home-made ornaments on both trees, as Paul strung the twinkling lights and Betty topped it off with tinsel icicles. They decided on an angel for the top of the living room tree, and a star to adorn the porch tree. That evening, in timely fashion, and thanks to the antenna on the roof that delivered CBS to their television set, they watched the second annual airing of "A Charlie Brown Christmas." They *just knew* the tree they had sought out and cut down had potential and were reminded that it just needed a little love.

Christmas traditions were important to Paul and Betty and they had already begun to put their ideas in place when Bonnie and Gail were toddlers. Paul started early setting up his train platform around their tree. He grew up in an area of Altoona called Logantown, which was a close-knit community of friends and relatives. Living in close proximity to the railroad shops, nearly everyone had at least one family member, neighbor or close friend who worked at the rail yards. Collecting model trains was a popular hobby among the folks there, and at Christmastime, many would create elaborate displays around their Christmas trees. The train tradition continued with the Nevels and their relatives as they grew up and had their own houses and families.

Paul had loved Christmas and the train displays for as long as he could remember. He recalled one Christmas in particular when he was allowed to play with the trains more than usual. It was the winter he contracted Scarlet Fever and almost died from the then-deadly disease. God had plans for that little boy, and he miraculously recovered. Playing with the trains was the one good memory he carried with him from that terrible experience.

When Paul worked for the PRR for a short time after he graduated from high school, he made what was good money at that time and one of his first purchases was his own train set. He bought a 1950 Lionel O-Gauge Diesel Engine 3-Unit Set. When he married Betty and left the homestead, he left most of his dad's trains and track for his brother Jake, as he planned to continue to build his own collection. Every year just after Thanksgiving, he would announce that it was time to begin working on setting up the train platform. The design changed a little each year, as it was a chance to be creative with layouts, adding a hill or a tunnel, and seeing what angles and curves the trains could handle. Piece by piece the collection grew to include houses, community buildings, figurines of people, animals, trees, snow, ponds and fences. The girls loved to play with the little pieces and create their own imaginary world as the villages and country scenes came to life.

They decorated inside and outside the house and went gift shopping when they could fit it in. On Christmas Eve, the family attended the Candlelight Service at the church and then went caroling with many of the church folk on a bus they rented for the occasion. They sang Christmas carols at a couple of nursing homes and the homes of church members who could not physically attend the service. It was such a joy to see their faces light up, especially when they saw the children and heard the singing and just knowing they were remembered. After caroling, the family drove to Betty and Buck's house for hot chocolate and cookies. Gram always had a red stocking for everyone in the family with each name carefully hand stitched in white needlepoint thread. She filled them with small gifts and a popcorn ball. Pap Pap added his gift of a Lifesaver Christmas Sweet Storybook for each girl. The girls were anxious to go home and wait for Santa Claus who would arrive at some point in the night, eat the cookies and drink the milk they sat out for him and deposit toys and gifts under the Christmas tree.

The first Christmas on the new farm was very meaningful, with Paul, Betty, Gram, Pap Pap and the four girls bundled up on a cold snowy morning around the Christmas tree in the living room, sharing joy and laughter. Even in the little house that was not ideal, they were experiencing the peace of God's gift of life and love.

Before opening gifts on Christmas morning, they had a time to remember and honor the true meaning of Christmas; that God so loved the world that He gave his only son, Jesus, whose birth we celebrate on Christmas. The girls would put together a little skit depicting some part of the Nativity or of its message. The older they grew, the more elaborate and creative their performances became. They would start to plan ahead as soon as the Christmas spirit enveloped them and kept their skit a secret to be revealed on Christmas morning. The anticipation became an important part of the tradition, and they enjoyed this part of the morning as much as anything else. Paul would read Luke's account of the story in Scripture, they sang their favorite carols, then lit a candle and sang happy birthday to Jesus. Finally, it was time for opening the gifts.

NINETEEN

For the Nevel girls and their cousins and friends, the barn on Asbury Lane was a large, mysterious shelter, sometimes hinting of danger, sometimes a place to play games like Cowboys and Indians, and hide and seek. If they were not looking for kittens buried in the hayloft, they were making tunnels with hay bales. They knew to stay out of the granary, a narrow room in the back of the barn that had its own door, which was always shut and usually locked. The floor boards in that room were not sturdy and some had rotted through. Paul did not want any of his kids or their friends to fall through into a horse stall below; besides there were hand tools and a variety of things in the room with which they could get into trouble. The kids heard his reasoning, but they still conjured up their own stories about the mysterious room with its many dangers, which made it into their make-believe adventures and tales.

The First Church of Christ's red brick building was another place where they spent quite a bit of time. It stood staunchly on the corner of 6th Avenue and 9th Street in Altoona. Parishioners could enter from either street and the avenue entrance had a long, wide cement staircase leading up to the front doors which made a great backdrop for Vacation Bible School and Sunday School class pictures. The dark brown wooden pews in the sanctuary were laid out in several sections on the deep red carpet, the largest section being a half circle in the middle. Beautiful stained glass windows etched with Bible characters and stories in vivid colors accented the encompassing walls. The wide stage was complete with a choir loft and baptistery. All in all, it created a reverent atmosphere in which to worship.

Sundays had always been a special day to Paul and Betty and a time in the 60s when most in America paused to reflect, worship and rest. The nation was not in such a hurry and the Lord's Day was considered sacred by many. Community league and school sports did not schedule competitions on Sundays and many stores and restaurants were closed.

After having children and moving to the farm, Sundays became a sometimes chaotic, yet favorite day of the week around the Nevel household. It started with lots of commotion as Betty woke the girls and fed them breakfast while Paul went to the barn to feed the horses. Then there was choosing which dresses to wear to church, usually a spat about who got the most time in front of the mirror in the bathroom and a reprimand that went something like, "Stop arguing, girls. Do you think God wants us to argue before we go to church?" By the time everyone was ready and out the door, Betty was exhausted and looking forward to a Sunday afternoon nap.

Church was a social as well as worshipful place. They greeted family and friends not seen for a week. Usually at least two of them sang in a choir on any given Sunday and they had those special Sunday School teachers they adored.

Julie especially loved Teacher Ruth's preschool class, where she and her cousins David (Glenn's son) and Patty (Jake's daughter) and friends Pennie and Ross were all together. Teacher Ruth always started class with songs she accompanied on her guitar. She would strum and sing, then the children would join in as they quickly learned the words and music. Ross always asked if they could sing "Fire Up!" and Teacher Ruth would start singing with a twinkle in her eye, "Fire up! Fire up! Christians fire up! Keep the fire burning in your soul, fire up!" The kids would start the song sitting down, then jump up into the air from their chairs each time they sang "Fire up!" Ruth figured it was a good way to burn off some of the kids' energy before the lesson. After a few songs, she would say a prayer and teach the weekly lesson. Sometimes she used flannel graphs to tell a Bible story, letting the kids take turns putting the flannel character cut outs on the flannel board. Other times there was a song that went with the story, like "Zacchaeus was a wee little man" or "The Lord said to Noah, 'You're gonna build an arky arky.'" Teacher Ruth loved Jesus and the kids could see it in her eyes and feel it in her warm hugs. She made them want to love Jesus, too.

Teacher Ruth knew she was planting seeds of faith in these children's lives, many of which would take root in fertile soil and be cultivated in their homes. What she could not have imagined was how God would make those seeds grow. She and their other teachers and mentors in the church were playing an important role in these young lives that would play out in world-impacting ways in years to come.

After visiting with friends and cousins following the service, often some of the last to leave the building, Paul and Betty would collect the children and head back to the farm.

The old station wagon was filled with chatter, sometimes overlapping, about what the girls learned in their classes, who was missing from church that day, how nice the choir sounded and who would be coming out to the farm later to visit. At home, the girls would change from their Sunday best into play clothes while Betty took the meat out of the oven and mashed the potatoes that had been soaking in water all morning. Bonnie and Gail would set the table. Buck and Betty Myers were regulars when the family gathered for Betty's scrumptious Sunday roast beef dinner. Besides the best mashed potatoes and gravy this side of heaven, there was corn from the garden in season, at times another vegetable and a side of garden salad or pickled eggs and beets. Betty's homemade sweet iced tea had no rival. As they took their places around the table and joined hands for prayer, Paul would ask, "Whose turn is it?" It was a family custom to take turns saying grace before their meals together. Paul always complimented Betty on her good cooking and because she felt appreciated, she never failed to keep those good meals coming.

After their bellies were full and the table was cleared, the girls headed outside to play, weather permitting. Almost every Sunday, friends or cousins or both would visit. In the summer, the kids would play kickball, take walks in the woods or bring the Barbies outside for a new adventure.

Betty, her mother and the ladies often played Scrabble or worked on putting a puzzle together. That was, until the girls begged Gram to take them to find treasures in the woods. She always responded with, "I'm sure I could use the exercise. Let's go see what we can find!"

Adventures in the woods with Gram were always delightful. She taught the kids to look for treasures in God's creation, such as all sizes of pine cones that she would use in her craft projects. They found rocks in the creek bed with fossils of worms and sea shells, and would imagine together how they might have ended up in the rocks. There was always a variety of wild flowers to collect and take home to put in a vase. Occasionally, they found edible treasures, such as wild raspberries, blackberries, strawberries, blueberries and cherries.

When other kids were visiting, they joined in the adventures, and Grandma Myers welcomed all of her grandkids' friends to also call her Gram.

At times when Paul and Betty were both working and Gram was not available to watch the kids, they would have one of the older cousins or teens from the church to babysit. The Nevel girls loved having babysitters, particularly their cousins Kathy, Cheryl or Sharon. With such a large extended family as well as their church family, Paul and Betty were rarely out of options for childcare. On one such summer day, Bonnie and Gail were especially excited when their cousin Randi was asked to look after them. Randi was just a few years older than Bonnie and the girls loved to spend time with her, as she was always fun and full of laughs.

That morning, Randi was getting breakfast for the girls and, as she picked Karen up to put her in her highchair, she asked Julie, "How about some Rice Krispies?"

"Sure," Julie replied. But only if she could pour her own.

Bonnie and Gail wanted toast with their mom's raspberry jelly. Randi was about to pour the milk for the cereal and said, "If you listen real close, you'll hear them go 'Crap, snackle, pop!'" As soon as it was out of her mouth, the girls looked a little surprised, then broke into a fit of laughter. Randi tried to correct her words to "Snap, crackle, pop," but it was too late. The new phrase would live on in infamy.

Just a little past Asbury Lane on the way to Bellwood was a local favorite ice cream stand called Sunny Crest. It was built of cement blocks painted yellow and offered various delicious ice cream flavors and sundaes. It was always a special treat to go there in the summers.

Randi's mom, whom the kids also loved and called Aunt Ethel, even though she was not technically their aunt, dropped Randi off for the day. After a busy morning of playing Barbies inside and swinging outside, Randi shared her idea that she had been thinking about.

"What do you girls think about going to Sunny Crest for ice cream cones?" The girls cheered. "Yay! We love Sunny Crest."

"I want chocolate peanut butter." Gail declared.

Julie danced around chanting, "Sunny Crest! Sunny Crest!"

Karen was only a year old and did not quite understand what all of the excitement was about, but she was smiling, too.

"But how will we get there, Randi?" asked Bonnie.

"We will walk." Randi answered. In Randi's mind, it was just down the road and around the corner. It did not seem far, at least when they passed it in the car. Besides, it was a beautiful sunny day and ice cream would be the perfect treat after getting some exercise.

In actuality, Sunny Crest was over a mile away from the house, which meant another mile home, mostly uphill. Karen was barely walking and would need to be carried most of the way. Julie was four years old and quite active, but had not yet gone on any two-mile hikes with steep hills involved. Randi realized about half-way there that she had misjudged the distance, but there was no turning back now, not with these girls dead-set on their reward for the walk being their favorite flavor of ice cream. That ice cream sure tasted good when they finally got there. How they got home, Randi said later, "Lord only knows." They all made it in one piece, only by the grace of God, according to Randi, as she half carried, half drug the little ones back up the lane.

Betty wondered why they were all exhausted when she got home. That is, until they told her about their excursion.

"You walked all the way to Sunny Crest?!" she exclaimed. "Poor Randi didn't know what she was getting into."

Randi was very sore for the next few days and the idea of walking to Sunny Crest never came up again, except to laugh about it over the years.

TWENTY

The summer when Bonnie was 11 years old was winding down when she invited her friend Linda to the farm for the weekend. The weather was perfect for them to play outside and groom the horses.

Shortly after Linda left on Sunday afternoon, Bonnie prepared to ride White Socks, the horse she claimed as her own, with the Riggles Gap Riding Club.

White Socks was a beautiful black quarter horse mare with white hair around each of her hooves. Bonnie had been faithfully brushing and grooming the horse, trying to do her part in taking care of the animal. Riggles Gap was at the other end of Asbury Lane and the club had Paul's permission to ride on the farm.

That Sunday, Paul saddled White Socks and Dusty and the younger kids waited their turn for rides. Paul and Glenn picked up the kids and helped them onto the horses. Then the men led them by their reins down the lane, back up and around the barn. After all of the little ones had a turn, the others with the riding club began to arrive on their horses. Soon they were ready for their adventure. Their leader Gary said, "Let's go to the orchard." Bonnie waved goodbye and off they went towards the woods. The younger kids lamented that they could not go too, but it did not take them long to get into a game of hide-n-seek.

The horseback riders were having a good jaunt through the woods with Bonnie, the youngest among them, holding her own. When they came to a clearing, they saw the orchard stretching out before them, row after row of apple trees deliciously decorated with clusters of red, shiny fruit. Some were riding close enough to pick an apple and have a taste. Bonnie followed suit and reached for one. She had to give a little extra tug when it did not snap off right away and White Socks kept going. Losing her balance, she tumbled backwards off the horse.

Several saw it happen, including Gary who was off his horse and beside her as quick as a flash. She hit her head on the ground and was very still for a moment. Gary's heart pounded, he breathed a quick prayer then assessed the situation. She looked a little woozy.

"Bonnie, hey Bon, are you okay?" he said and patted her cheek softly.

She looked at him with a blank stare. She tried to sit up but he dared not let her.

"Wait, take it easy there... Are you hurt? What hurts?"

By now the other riders had gathered around. Bonnie knew she had fallen and that her head hurt and her pride hurt, but otherwise she did not feel like anything was broken.

"I think I'm okay. I'm so sorry to hold everyone up. Is White Socks okay?" She saw something in her hand and smiled. "Oh, wow I held on to the apple. It better taste good, hope it was worth it."

Everyone laughed and the group sighed a collective sigh of relief. It seemed like she was fine. After a break and munching their apples, they mounted their horses again. Bonnie was a little nervous as Gary helped her get onto White Socks. But as an experienced rider, he knew the best thing was for her to get right back on.

White Socks was also a little spooked from the whole episode, but she stood still as Gary gently stroked her and calmly talked to her, "Easy, girl, easy. It's okay. Good girl. You have precious cargo here."

Gary had the group head back and made sure he rode close beside Bonnie.

Just when Paul was thinking it was time for the riders to be coming back, he spotted the group as they appeared emerging from the woods.

The younger kids were still playing outside and he and Jake had been tinkering around in the barn. When they got closer, Paul shouted, "Here come the cowboys! How was the ride? Oh, and the cowgirls."

Gary hopped down to talk to Paul. "Well, we had a little incident..." And proceeded to tell him what happened.

They helped Bonnie off of White Socks and she looked a little pale. Paul tried not to sound alarmed, realizing things could have been much worse.

He looked her in the eyes, "Honey, are you okay?"

Bonnie tried to smile but she was not feeling too good. "My head hurts, Dad. I fell. It was not White Socks' fault though."

She sat down in the grass and by now Betty suspected that something was wrong and ran out.

"Let me see your head. I bet it hurts right there." She felt a lump on the back of Bonnie's head. "Let's go in and get some ice on that."

They started toward the house.

"Linda's mom called to thank us for having Linda and said she had a real nice time. Did you enjoy your time with her? She's such a sweet girl; I'm glad you've been able to keep in touch."

Bonnie glanced at her mother. "Who?"

"Linda, her mom called while you were riding."

"I don't know what you mean. Linda? Who is Linda?"

Betty and Paul exchanged looks of concern.

"I'll get the car, we're taking her to the hospital," he said, heading toward the station wagon.

After examining Bonnie in the Emergency Room, it was determined that she should spend the night in the hospital. It made Betty worry even more, but the doctor reassured her it was for observation and to err on the side of caution. The little girl definitely had a concussion from the fall and they wanted to make sure there were no after-effects.

Paul and Betty left the other kids with Jake and Mary at the farm. Paul said he would go home to tend to the girls and leave Betty to spend the night in the hospital with Bonnie. It was a long, restless night for Betty as she tried to doze in a chair but could never really fall asleep. Nurses made their rounds and took turns waking Bonnie every hour to make sure she was responding and doing okay.

The young patient was very sleepy and complained of a headache and nausea. Sometimes she would ask where she was and why, but would drift back off to sleep before she could make sense of the answers. Betty just kept alternating between worry and prayer, worry and prayer. Even though Paul was at home in his own bed, he did not sleep much better than his wife. He could not shut off the what-ifs that were racing through his mind.

Staring up at the dark ceiling, he ran the gauntlet, whispering, "Maybe I shouldn't have let her go. Maybe the saddle wasn't tight enough. What if there's permanent damage? Oh dear Lord, please oh, please protect my little girl and heal her, God."

The doctor's visit to Bonnie's room the next day could not have come soon enough for Betty. He did a thorough exam and decided she was well enough to go home, as long as they kept an eye on her and followed precautions. She still did not remember the incident or the ride back to the barn, but she knew where she was at that moment and was able to recall the events of previous days.

Glenn picked Betty and Bonnie up at the hospital and took them to the farm. On the way, he asked Bonnie, "How are you feeling, Eve?"

She giggled and replied, "You're trying to trick me, Uncle Glenn. I'm doing better and I know my name is Bonnie."

He had a twinkle in his eye as he said, "Well, you're Eve to me now, because you remind me of another lady who got into trouble when she picked an apple and it caused a great fall."

It would be a few years before Bonnie fully appreciated the joke.

Paul and the girls were waiting and ran to the car when it pulled up. They all wanted to help Bonnie get out of the car and had her bed all ready for her. For several days, she was the center of attention for the family. In fact, the doctor had ordered bedrest for her for the next few days and she did not mind at all having her little sisters wait on her hand and foot. She was feeling a little better each day, hoping to be fine by the time school started in a week.

Paul and Betty were greatly relieved to see her progress, though naturally they were still concerned. "Do you think she'll ever want to ride again?" Betty wondered aloud to Paul.

Paul answered, "I guess we'll see. I think it would be good for her to get back on a horse, but gone are the days of me letting her ride off alone. I'm just glad she was with adults who could help get her back home when she fell."

A week passed and Bonnie was getting back to her old self when she asked, "Can I go to the barn with you, Dad? I want to see White Socks. I don't want her to think I'm mad at her."

"Sure, Bon," said Paul. "I think that's a good idea, if you're up for it."

They walked to the barn and Paul called the horses in from the pasture. If they were close enough to see him walking toward the barn, they would often beat him there. If they were further away over the hill, he would clang the old cowbell that had been left in the barn by the Kutruffs. Even after grazing all day, they were always ready for their grain, which Bonnie liked to divvy out from the old wooden grain box.

As she opened the latch and lifted the heavy lid, Gail and Julie came around the corner. Julie was holding a calico kitten she had scooped up just inside the barn. They had seen Bonnie and their dad walking to the barn and wanted to be there to witness Bonnie seeing White Socks again. The horses filed in through the doors and the back hallway into their respective stalls. Bonnie went right to White Socks and began to talk to her and stroke her face and neck. White Socks nuzzled up to her as if to offer an apology.

"It's okay, girl, I'm okay. I know you didn't mean for me to fall off, it was my own fault. No more picking apples when I'm riding you."

"Does that mean you will ride again? Will you be scared?" Gail asked innocently.

"Well I rode back down here after I fell, at least that's what they tell me, I still don't remember it. But dad said he thinks I should try it so I won't always be afraid."

Julie thought to herself that her big sister sure was brave. Maybe the bravest person she knew.

"I'll be scared to death," Bonnie admitted. "But Dad will help me; he won't let me fall."

Another week went by before Paul was ready to encourage Bonnie to ride. He wanted to teach her to be brave, as there are many instances in life and faith that call for it. He learned about bravery as a child when he watched his father determined to provide for his family in the midst of the Great Depression. He learned to bravely face many adversities in the Army throughout basic training and even more so in his time overseas. He had a small taste of having to step up to take the high road with those like the hardened master sergeant who considered the choirboys with a small amount of contempt. He learned to call up courage to stand against evil in those who had brought war to the Korean people and made orphans of innocent little children.

It was hard to be a father, but there were times that fathers had to be brave in teaching their children to have courage.

However, Betty was not ready for it. "I'll stay in the house, thank you," she said. "Please be careful."

Steeling himself, Paul held Bonnie's hand as they walked toward the barn.

"You can brush her while I get the saddle pad and saddle ready. Do you know what John Wayne said once? 'Courage is being scared to death... and saddling up anyway.'" Bonnie thought about that for a moment. She liked it.

When it was time, Paul said, "You ready for this, Bon? I'll help you up and won't let go."

She was feeling butterflies in her stomach but did not want to disappoint her dad so she tried to put on a brave face. She put her left foot in the stirrup as her dad lifted her partway and helped her swing her right leg over White Sock's back.

"Steady, girl," Paul said to the horse. "Here Bonnie, hold onto the reins."

"Wait, dad! Don't let go!"

"I won't honey, I have you, just take the reins. We'll just stay here for a bit. She knows you're not sure, let's let you both get used to each other for a few minutes."

Bonnie held on for dear life. "I don't know about this, Dad. I'm scared, maybe..."

"You're fine, honey, I've got you. I promise. Take a deep breath...."

It was at that moment that Bonnie saw her sisters walking toward them from the house.

"Hurray, Bon, you're on," shouted Gail.

"Go Bonnie, go," Julie said followed with, "Yee haw!"

Their encouragement gave her courage and Bonnie said, "Okay, Dad, let's try a few steps. Slowly. Take it slow."

"You're in charge," said Paul. "White Socks will follow your lead."

He walked beside her, keeping his hand on her. They walked by the other girls who were still cheering her on and Paul winked at them. Sometimes, brave fathers have their moments.

TWENTY-ONE

Julie and her cousin David, being the young farmers they believed they were, had asked for cowboy boots for their birthdays when they were turning five years old. David's birthday was in April, so he got his first and Julie could hardly wait for July to come. When she got her beautiful new brown leather cowboy boots, she could not have been more proud. She wanted to wear them with everything from her bathing suit to her dresses, and insisted on wearing them to bed. Paul swore she had found some of his super glue and glued them to her feet.

With cowboy boots now a part of the adventures, hide and seek in the woods with Gram often turned into Cowboys and Indians, with cap guns and play bow-and-arrows. They played in the woods until fall turned to colder days with winter on the horizon. Then it was sleds and snow balls and snowmen.

"Girls, I'm leaving in half an hour for the shower," called Betty. "I expect you to help your dad with watching your little sisters."

"Oh, but Mom," whined Gail, "we are busy. We were just planning Ken and Barbie's vacation and we need…"

"We need our space," Bonnie chimed in. "Julie won't leave our Barbies alone. Can't she go with you?"

Gail countered with, "No, take Karen. She pulled off Midge's arm yesterday."

There were times when Betty felt like she was a referee in some long-running kid's game.

"Now girls, I can't take the little ones with me, and they will be fine. It's up to you two to be a good example and play nicely. I'll set them up over in this corner with their own Barbies." Betty unfolded the little plastic doll house and hoped it would humor Julie and Karen for a little while at least.

"If you're good, you can all have a bed time snack at 8:30 before Dad puts you to bed."

She had a predictable formula for dealing with them; the carrot and the stick. Start with the carrot but never forget the stick.

"I made chocolate chip cookies this morning," she said with a smile, then turned stern. "But if your father hears you bickering, you will go to bed at 8:30 and no snack. Do you understand?"

Four heads bobbed up and down to the tune of "Yes, Mommy. Okay, Mommy." They knew if they did not agree, they would get *the look* and they narrowly escaped it. *The look* usually preceded a serious reprimand or punishment or, worse, telling Dad.

The girls busied themselves with their Barbies after their mother left. They loved to dress them up in the various outfits Gram had crocheted just for the dolls, which were sprawled out all over the living room floor.

Paul sat in the rocking chair reading the Saturday issue of the Altoona Mirror. Karen retreated to his lap just long enough to interrupt, then crawled back down on the floor for more Barbie adventures.

"What an unusually quiet evening," Paul thought to himself as he smiled, peering over the top of his newspaper to watch his girls play. They were actually getting along and their doll talk was quite creative. It was getting close to snack time and it looked as if they had earned it.

Paul went to the back bedroom for a few minutes to see if Betty had left the girls' pajamas out and ready for them. Of course she had. There they were, adorable warm pj's for each of the girls laid out on their beds. It occurred to him that he better check the furnace, as it was a cold winter night and the temperature would continue to drop. As he draped on his old work coat, he said, "Bonnie, I'm going to check the furnace. I'll be right back. Why don't you girls start cleaning up and putting things away? Then you can put your jammies on."

"Aw, Daddy, but we're not done with…"

"Do you want those cookies your mom made for you?"

"Hmm…" The oldest was about to attempt to negotiate when she remembered the carrot waiting. "Oh yeah, okay, c'mon guys let's clean up."

Paul went out the front door and around to the side of the house to the cellar door. He hadn't realized it had started snowing. With thick work gloves on, he unlatched the furnace door only to see the coal was glowing red hot. He threw in another shovel full of coal and thought that should be enough to keep the house warm for the night. Then he shoveled up some ashes from around the furnace and took them outside to scatter on the snow and ice where Betty would be parking the car and walking back to the house.

He hoped the snow did not keep up or she would not want to drive. She would rather spend the night on a church pew than brave even a light Pennsylvania snow, he jokingly thought to himself. All of Betty's family and friends knew how she hated to drive in the snow or be in a car with someone else driving in the snow. And, if she had her way and could stay put while it was snowing, she would still be worried about whoever might happen to be out there driving in the inclement weather. All winter plans were in deference to her famous line, "If it doesn't snow."

All joking aside, Paul whispered a prayer that God would see her safely home. When they were merely a few steps apart or many, many miles, Paul and Betty never ceased praying for each other and their families. It was a habit of their lives that never changed, never wavered and only grew stronger.

While Paul was outside, the girls were dutifully putting their Barbies and their accessories away and even little Karen watched her sisters and followed suit, not wanting to be left out. It became a game now to see who could get their jammies on first. Julie, however, decided that she was thirsty and needed a drink of water. Being only five years old, she was not tall enough to reach the kitchen spigot, so she had concocted her own way of getting up to get a drink. She would jump up and balance herself at the waist on the edge of the sink then lean forward to turn on the water. The couple of times her mother had caught her doing it, she got a quick scolding. "Next time I catch you jumping up there like that, Julie Sue, you will get a spanking. You could fall right off and get hurt." Well no one was around and all that mattered to Julie Sue at the moment was getting that cool drink of well water at the kitchen sink.

She saw a pink plastic cup on the counter that she would use. She jumped up, balanced herself, and reached for the cup. Just as quickly, she lost her balance and fell forward, her right hand going into the sink with all of her weight behind it. But instead of hitting the bottom of the sink, there was a glass sitting there that caught all of her forward momentum. It broke under her hand. The next thing Julie knew was that she saw blood streaming up from her hand and all around. She wondered which hand she had cut and let out a scream.

Her sisters ran in from the bedroom and her father bolted through the front door where they found little Julie Sue standing with her feet back down on the floor, wide eyed and holding her hands up.

Paul yelled to Bonnie, "Get me a rag, a cloth, a blanket, one of your doll baby blankets! Hurry!"

Gail ran as fast as she could to the bedroom and back, bringing a baby blanket to her dad. He quickly made a tourniquet around Julie's right wrist, struggling to remain calm.

"Bonnie, run across the road to the Kutruffs and ask if we can borrow their car. Tell them what happened. Hurry honey."

He scooped up Julie in his arms and told her to try to hold her hand upright as much as she could.

Mr. Kutruff heard a loud rapping on his door, and could not imagine who would be knocking at this time of night and in the middle of a snowstorm, no less. Mrs. Kutruff beat him to the door where Bonnie stood shivering and out of breath and trying to say something.

"Oh my, come in out of the cold, dear, where's your coat? What is wrong, honey? Slow down now; tell me what's the matter…?"

"It's Julie, she cut her hand, it's bleeding everywhere," Bonnie said. "Daddy said to ask, to see if we could - if he could maybe borrow your car? I think he needs to take her to the hospital. Mom's not home, she has the car, it's snowing, she doesn't know…"

Mr. Kutruff was already reaching for the keys and grabbing his jacket off the coat rack by the door. "C'mon with me."

Paul was hurriedly walking toward the Kutruff house carrying Julie.

Mrs. Kutruff had Bonnie by the hand and passing the frantic father assured him saying, "I'll stay here with them, go on now, we'll be fine."

Paul quickly climbed in the back seat with Julie so that he would have room to hold her and Mr. Kutruff turned the key to start the car. The engine barely turned over and stopped. He turned it again and it sounded like it would start, but it stopped again, hampered by the cold night air. Silence. Big snowflakes drifted down over the car in slow motion. Even Julie was silent. In fact, she had been pretty calm throughout the ordeal so far.

"Paul, I'm so sorry, the ole' Cadillac doesn't do so well in cold temps," said Mr. Kutruff.

He tried to start it again, to no avail.

Paul was trying not to panic. The tourniquet seemed to be holding the bleeding at bay, but he knew it was a bad cut and they needed to get to the hospital.

"Okay, to the truck!" cried Mr. Kutruff with a sudden burst of inspiration.

"That old thing?" Paul thought, but it was worth a try. He breathed a prayer that God would cause it to start as they scampered to the truck behind Mr. Kutruff's garage.

The old red pickup truck was a '52 Ford that Mr. Kutruff had held onto to use around the farm, but it hadn't gotten much use since the Nevels took over the farm. As if by a miracle, the truck turned over the first time and they were on their way. Mr. Kutruff did his best to hurry on snow-covered roads, but Paul thought it was the slowest ride in the slowest old truck he could ever imagine.

All he could do was pull Julie's coat around her and hold her close, trying to keep her warm and calm.

"Honey, you are such a brave little girl," he whispered, his mouth close to her ear. "I know it has to hurt so bad, but it's going to be alright. We'll soon have a doctor look at it."

For her part, Julie just snuggled into her dad and decided she was going to make him proud and be brave.

Though the hand throbbed, she kept thinking about how much trouble she was in for jumping up to the sink.

"So, how did this happen, anyway?" asked her father, trying to keep her mind off the pain.

"I was thirsty, Dad. I'm sorry," she said and choked back the tears. "Daddy, am I in big trouble?"

Paul kissed her head, "Uh, no sweetie. I think you learned your lesson and next time you'll ask for help, right?"

But Paul was worried that her little hand and fingers might be the ones in big trouble. He silently prayed, "Dear God, please save her hand, please give us the right doctors, please get us there safely."

Meanwhile, it was a rare evening out without kids for Betty and she had a wonderful time with the ladies at the shower. Things were beginning to wrap up and glancing at her watch, she pictured the girls getting their pajamas on, and having cookies and milk around the kitchen table. She had instructed Paul about the cookies, which she made as much for him as for the girls since they were his favorite. She knew he would sneak a few for himself after the girls were in bed.

Someone calling her name interrupted her thoughts. "Betty, there's a call for you in the church office, it's your neighbor."

Betty always left a number where she could be reached by phone when she left the house on these occasions.

"My neighbor? Why would she be calling? Oh no, I hope nothing bad has happened…"

She hurried to the office and picked up the receiver. "Hello?"

"Betty, this is Mrs. Kutruff. First of all, please know we are all okay. I'm here with your girls and Paul is with Mr. Kutruff taking Julie to the hospital. She fell and cut her hand."

"What?! The hospital??"

In reality, Betty's neighbor did not know how serious the injury was but there was no reason to unduly worry her. "Yes, but it's just precautionary, there was some bleeding and she probably needs a few stitches."

Betty's stomach turned at the thought. "Oh my goodness, I'm so glad you called. I'm not far from the hospital and I'll just head over and meet them there. Thank you."

The concerned mother was already headed to the door and poor Mrs. Kutruff was left on the other end of a line that went dead.

She ran back to the fellowship hall and quickly grabbed her things, thanking the ladies for a lovely evening, and apologizing for leaving so abruptly. She called back over her shoulder, "Please pray for Julie, she cut her hand and probably needs stitches. Paul's on his way to the hospital with her."

Reaching the big wooden door that led out to the street where her car was parked, she wrapped her scarf closely around her neck before she hit the cold air. She was taken aback as she stepped out and saw it had been snowing. "Oh no, not snow!" Within minutes, she had gone from laughing and eating and playing games with the ladies, to facing her two greatest fears; driving in the snow, and one of her girls being hurt.

About the time Betty was climbing in behind the steering wheel, Mr. Kutruff pulled up to the Emergency entrance at the Altoona Hospital.

Almost before the old truck stopped, Paul was out and carrying Julie through the doors. "Please someone, help. Please get a doctor right away!"

In retrospect, he later felt a bit foolish. However, a concerned father could not be blamed for appearing slightly crazy when his little girl was in trouble.

Minutes later, Julie was on a stretcher being wheeled down the hall and Paul was right behind her. When they got her into a room, a doctor carefully unwound the tourniquet and inspected the damage.

"Good move, Dad. Did you do this?" the doctor asked. "You saved your little girl from losing a lot of blood and maybe saved her hand from further damage."

The doctor held up Gail's doll blanket which was soaked in deep red. He must have recognized it as belonging to Julie and possibly important. "Do you want to keep this?"

"Um…" It was the last thing on Paul's mind. "No thanks, it'll be too hard to clean up, just throw it away."

Julie watched the blanket being tossed into a trash can and felt a little sad for Gail. And a little sad for herself, since it was all her fault.

The Altoona Hospital Emergency Room medical team went to work on anesthetizing and delicately stitching closed the gaping wound in Julie's little hand.

With her dad at her side, she was still trying to be brave but at the same time was very curious. When she would lift her head to watch, the nurse would gently push it back down. She tried again, thinking it could not be so bad, why could she not watch? The nurse shook her head no and pushed her head back down again. The more the nurse tried to prevent her from seeing, the more determined she was to tough it out and not cry.

When they were done, they wheeled her into a recovery room where a nervous Betty was waiting impatiently to see her. Ironically, she was so worried about Julie while driving to the hospital that she barely had a chance to worry about the snow on the road.

The doctor gave the parents an optimistic diagnosis of Julie's chances for a full recovery. Yet, Betty's stomach turned a little at seeing the big white bandage wrapped around her little girl's hand and arm.

"Oh Julie, my goodness. Poor girl. Does it hurt?"

"It's okay, Mom…" In an odd case of role reversal, Julie was calmer than her mother.

"Is it true you were jumping up to the sink, like I've told you so many times not to?" And there it was, the dreaded look. Julie knew it; she just knew she was in big trouble.

"Yes, but Mom, everyone was busy and I needed a drink of water. Please don't be mad, Mom!" A tear slipped out and she quickly wiped it away with her good hand.

Betty's stern tone fell away with the tear. "I hear you've been a very brave girl."

Julie nodded and swallowed hard, trying to hold back any more tears. Suddenly she was feeling very sleepy and felt herself drifting off.

"They gave her a shot with some pretty good pain medicine," Paul explained to Betty. "The doctor said we can take her home as soon as they make sure she's not going to have any bad reactions to anything they gave her. He also said the next couple of days will be a lot more painful for her. They stitched everything back together as carefully as possible. There were some nerves and tendons involved and only time will tell if anything's been permanently damaged."

The thought of that possibility made Betty's stomach turn once again, as she leaned into Paul and felt a little faint. "Oh let's pray there's not any major damage. She's only five, this could affect the rest of her life."

Paul pulled her close and said, "We'll make sure we find the best doctor to follow up with and hope and pray for the best."

Though Paul and Betty tossed and turned all night, awakened by the slightest noise, Julie slept soundly through the night, thanks to the pain medicine still in her system.

But morning brought another story. The pain predicted by the emergency room doctor hit. Paul held Julie on his lap in the rocking chair and soothed her with his soft humming. "It's okay to cry now, honey. You are still my brave little girl. Go ahead and cry, just let it go. I know it has to hurt so bad. That's it, baby, let it go."

With the rising sun, the roads began to clear. Betty decided to take the other three girls to church and Paul stayed home with Julie. A quiet house might just be what their little injured girl needed, and a good worship service might just be what her mom needed.

A few days later, the worst of the pain had subsided and they agreed it was time for Julie to go back to school.

"I'm ready, Mom, I want to go," she told a reluctant mother.

They stood in front of the closet looking for a dress with a sleeve that would fit over her big white bandage that looked like a cast. Betty chose a blue dress with puffy white sleeves and elastic that would slip over the large dressing. She drove Julie to school and walked in with her so she could talk to the teacher.

"It's very important that she's careful not to bump it or get run into or anything. And no matter how much she begs, no recess, please," Betty explained to Mrs. Henry.

"Class, class! Time to find your desk and sit down. Quiet everyone, quiet." Mrs. Henry paused as the kindergartners took their seats and a hush fell over the room. Then they noticed Julie standing in the front of the classroom with the teacher's arm around her.

"First of all, let's welcome Julie back after her absence." They applauded. Julie blushed.

"She's had an accident and her hand still has lots of healing to do. Everyone must be very careful to not bump into her and to help watch out for her while we're at school. Is that understood class? Can we be good helpers?"

Betty smiled as she heard a collective "Yes, Mrs. Henry." She waved a thank you to the teacher from outside the door and walked away down the hall.

Lori was one of Julie's new friends in her kindergarten class. She had short brown hair that flipped up on the ends and an adorable smile that matched her friendly disposition. Their desks were side by side, and each girl noticing the kindness of the other, they had an instant bond on the first day of school. Lori was worried when Julie did not come to class for a few days. She was so glad to see her come in the morning of her return that she ran to hug her. Seeing that big white bandage on her hand, Lori's heart went out to Julie. After Mrs. Henry had asked the class to welcome Julie back, Lori raised her hand and volunteered to be her special helper.

"Why Lori, that's very kind of you," said Mrs. Henry as she walked over to her desk and bent down to look her in the eye. "Yes, you can be her helper. She will need help as she can't do some things with just one hand. Thank you very much."

Julie sat down at her desk and looked at Lori and smiled.

Eventually, it was time to take Julie back to the hospital to have her hand examined and the stitches removed. Julie was anxious to see what her hand looked like under all those bandages and Betty coaxed her to be brave. As the doctor began to unwrap the dressings, Betty saw that poor little shriveled up hand and the black stitches protruding from the wounded area and promptly felt extremely queasy.

Julie looked over at her mother saying, "Look, Mom. Doesn't it look funny?" But her mother had a strange look on her face and it was not *the look*.

The room became very warm, Betty's eyes rolled back in her head and she slumped down in her chair. One of the nurses held Julie's hand still while the doctor and the other nurse hurried over to keep Betty from slipping onto the floor.

"She just passed out," the little girl heard someone say.

So there lay Julie on one examination table and her mother beside her on another.

"She told me to be brave," Julie remarked innocently to the nurse beside her. "I guess I'm gonna have to be brave all by myself."

"It's fine, sweetie," replied the nurse. "Sometimes seeing stitches can make some people, especially mothers, just a little sick in their tummies."

Not really understanding what was happening, the little girl was frightened to see her mom pass out cold. And although Betty insisted that she would be okay, the nurses did not let her get up until they were done with their patient. Unfortunately, the doctor decided that the hand was not sufficiently healed for the stitches to come out yet. He put ointment on it and re-wrapped it.

The physician said to Betty, "It's healing nicely, but let's give it another week. This time I'd like for the bandages to be changed every two days and, um..." He offered her a weak smile, "Is there someone else besides you who could do that?"

Paul's sister Myra Sue, "Aunt Susie" to the girls, lived just a few blocks from the hospital. When she got the call to ask if she could offer assistance, she was happy to oblige. She had moved to California when she married her husband George. He died tragically at a young age, leaving her with three young boys, John, Jim and Allen. Myra Sue moved back to Altoona and her family was glad to have her back in the area.

Although the day had started out as Julie being the patient, Betty was the one who spent the rest of the day on Myra Sue's couch. The boys were in school and Julie played a little with her cousins' toys, though she did not really feel much like playing. The day had been disappointing; she still had her stitches and a big bandage, her hand really hurt and her mother looked really sick.

Later that evening after they put the girls to bed, Betty sat down beside Paul on the couch and said, "Honey, I'm really worried about Julie's hand. It looked awful."

Paul noticed the color going out of her face and put his arm around her. "Now, now, no more thinking about how it looked or I'll have to carry you to bed."

"It was bad, Paul," Betty continued. "The doctor recommended that we take her to a specialist to see if she'll need surgery. He couldn't be sure of what permanent damage might have been done. I just wish I would've stayed home that night, maybe it wouldn't have happened."

"Honey, you can't keep thinking that way. I could just as easily blame myself. It was an accident and it's done now. We just have to keep praying that it will heal completely and for wisdom to choose the best course of action."

While Betty appreciated her husband's logical wisdom, she knew it would be hard not to worry in the coming days.

Pap Pap was the one who tended to the bandages and dressings for the next week and Julie enjoyed sitting on his lap and getting all of his attention.

Julie's Great Aunt Vada, another one of the Rudasill fifteen, took her to her next checkup. It was decided Betty was better off left at home. The hand had healed enough and this time the stitches could come out. Julie thought her scar was very fascinating. She showed it off to anyone who would look, though it was still very sore and tender to the touch. She thought it was kind of neat that she could put her hand under steaming hot water without it burning, and pick up the hot toast right out of the toaster with her right hand when it was too hot for anyone else to handle. Her mother was not amused.

With the stitches removed, they visited a specialist who did various tests on Julie's hand and fingers. Betty's most important concern and question for the doctor was, "If you don't do surgery, will she still be able to play the piano and type on a typewriter?"

The specialist could not guarantee it 100%, but he believed she would. He did not think surgery would increase the odds much and his expert opinion was that the nerves and tendons would continue to heal. The bodies of children have a remarkable healing quality about them and he expected that the patient would regain full use of her hand. It would just take some time.

Betty prayed that God would heal that little hand completely, and that Julie indeed would be able to play the piano and type. She had no idea what God had in store for her little girl, but she believed He had a plan for her life, as she believed He did for all of her girls.

TWENTY-TWO

The end of August rolled around and it was Julie's turn to start first grade. She had done well in kindergarten, going half days, and now she would be in class full days. Bonnie was an eighth grader in the junior/senior high school, and Gail was starting her last year in grade school, sixth grade. Betty hated to see her girls growing up so quickly and though the first day of school was always an exciting day, she had mixed emotions as she helped the girls get ready that morning.

Paul left for work about the time they were waking up, so he kissed each one good-bye and told them that he would look forward to hearing about their day at dinner that night.

They had shopped for new outfits and were looking their best. So as to not make little three-year-old Karen feel left out, she got a new outfit, too.

The bus stop was almost a mile away. Betty drove the girls down the lane and to their stop. She sent them off with hugs and kisses. Before the girls boarded, she told Gail, "Watch out for your little sister, please. I know you'll want to sit with your friends, but just make sure she's okay."

"Okay, Mom, I will," Gail replied and rolled her eyes. Mothers, they were always complicating grownup girls' lives.

Karen wanted to go along on the bus, too, but had to settle with waving good-bye through the car window.

It was exciting for Julie to ride the bus with the older kids. She felt so grown up and mature.

Betty prayed for their protection and good learning experiences as she watched the girls get on their respective buses and be whisked away in a blur of yellow. Or maybe it was the tears that caused the blur.

When they arrived at their building, Gail walked Julie to her classroom and said, "Here you are, Jules. You're a big girl now, going into first grade. You'll love it. Have a great first day."

However, Julie did not want to let go of her hand. "C'mon, you'll be fine, you'll see. I'll meet you right here when school's over and walk you to the bus. Okay?"

Julie nodded as Gail pulled her hand gently away and waved, then she hurried down the hall. The new first grader felt a lump in her throat. Just when a tear started to well up in her eye, she looked around the classroom and there sat Lori! Her face brightened, as she saw her friend was in the same class with her again. Suddenly, first grade did not seem so scary.

Their teacher was Mrs. Tyler and they soon were learning their other classmates' names. A girl named Cathy sat behind Julie and across from Lori. The three of them were a little shy with each other at first, but they would become fast friends in the days ahead.

They began the day with pledging allegiance to the American flag. Julie was embarrassed that she couldn't always remember her right from her left, then discovered she had a little crutch to remember by; she would glance at her hand to see which one had the big scar from her accident with the glass and subsequent stitches. She knew that was her right hand, so that was the one to place over her heart. She wondered if anyone else in her class had such a handy aid or if they just instinctively knew their right from their left. She had, of course, learned the Pledge of Allegiance in kindergarten.

They learned a new song, "My Country 'Tis of Thee." Mrs. Tyler told her students that they would begin school each day with the pledge and the song, followed by a moment of silence. Julie guessed that was a time to pray because prayer time was about the only time at her house that it was completely silent, unless everyone was sleeping.

Every student's favorite time of the day was lunch then recess where Julie, Cathy and Lori gravitated toward one another. They sat at the same table and ate their packed lunches, sometimes trading or sharing an apple or bag of potato chips or a peanut butter and jelly sandwich. Julie and her sisters were allowed to buy the cafeteria lunch two days a week, if they liked what was on the menu. Julie loved her new metal lunch box with a red handle, featuring the cartoon characters from Banana Splits. Lori's was Chitty Chitty Bang Bang, and Cathy had Snoopy on hers. It was always fun every year before school started to shop for a new lunch box. After lunch the class went outside for recess, weather permitting. They played with big red kick balls, climbed on the monkey bars, on the days they were not wearing dresses, and swung on the swings, seeing who could go the highest. The three girls did well with their school work and playing with others.

Picture day was a big day for everyone. All of the teachers hoped for their class to be called early in the day so they could have their students looking fresh, with hair in place, before they had a chance to go outside to recess and ruin their neatness. Betty helped her girls pick out a favorite dress, put barrettes in their hair then lined them up in the living room for a picture. She sent a comb to school with each of them.

When Mrs. Tyler's class was called for the photo sessions, they were expected to line up and file quietly down the hallway. The first time, Julie felt butterflies in her stomach as she watched her classmates go one by one and sit on the stool while the photographer's assistant helped them pose, turning their chins a little this way and tilting their heads a little that way. She hoped she would smile enough for her mom's liking. School photos were anxious moments.

When it was Julie's turn, the photographer said, "Show us those pretty dimples." That made her smile, revealing the creases in her cheeks. She was relieved when it was over.

The timing of the first grade school pictures proved fortuitous, in retrospect.

The next weekend when Julie and Karen were getting their Saturday evening bath, Betty was on the phone in the kitchen when she heard a loud noise in the bathroom. Julie was getting cold and was ready to get out of the tub. She thought she could do it on her own and did not wait for her mother. As she stepped out, she slipped and fell hard, hitting her mouth against the porcelain bath tub. As she got up, she felt her lips and oops…something did not feel right. In fact, her front tooth felt jagged. Oh no, she had broken her front tooth! And there was the piece that broke off, lying on the floor. She picked it up and walked out to tell her mom.

Betty would have dropped the phone had she not already finished the conversation with her mother and had just placed the receiver on the cradle. "Julie! What happened?"

"I fell…" Julie smiled an embarrassed smile. Betty saw her broken tooth in her smile and the other half in her hand as Julie reached it out to show her.

"Oh no! Not your new tooth! It just came in, and so nicely." Betty began to cry as she sat down at the kitchen table and pulled Julie up on her lap.

"Mom, I'm okay, it doesn't hurt." Julie could not understand why her mom was crying when it was her tooth.

"Are you sure? Well hopefully it didn't damage the nerve then, we can be thankful for that. But your pretty new tooth. I can't believe it. It's such a shame. I'll have to call the dentist on Monday."

The next day in church and at school on Monday, Julie was self-conscious about smiling. She was afraid that she looked silly. But when the dentist examined her and said he could build a partial tooth and use a material that would bond to what was left of the tooth, it would be good as new. Well, almost. But it did the trick.

❧

September flew by and the woods around the farm began to change color. Vibrant green leaves turned to shades of yellow, orange, and red. One day Lori was missing from class. Then she was out the next day.

Cathy and Julie wondered where she could be. "Maybe she caught the flu," Cathy speculated. The flu was a catch-all illness that explained most illnesses for kids. The flu and a cold; this person or that person had the flu or they had a cold.

That evening Betty sat down with Julie and said she had some sad news. "Honey, I got a call from a friend of Lori's family. There was a bad car accident. Lori is okay, she wasn't in the car. But her daddy was hurt real bad and they couldn't save him. He's in heaven now, sweetie. Her mom and sister are injured, but they will be okay."

"Oh no, poor, poor Lori. Her daddy died? Why, mom? Why did she have to lose her dad?"

Betty comforted her as best as she could. How she hated for her children to have to learn about the unfair cruelties of a harsh world, but she knew this was part of life and a teachable moment. "There are things that happen that we just can't explain, honey. It's so sad and it seems unfair. I don't know why. But God does and we just have to trust Him that he'll take care of Lori and her family."

"Where is Lori, Mom, if her parents aren't with her?"

"She's with her grandparents," Betty explained.

"Her Mam and Pap? I saw them at her birthday party. They're nice." Julie thought about it a moment. "Will she get to come back to our school?"

"I'm sure she will honey. And when she does, she'll need a good friend."

Julie nodded, wiping away a tear that had trickled down her cheeks. "Wonder what heaven is like?"

"I wonder, too. We know it's better than anything we can imagine and we won't have to be sad anymore. Lori's dad is in a better place than any of us are down here. Lori will see him again someday. But for now, it will be very hard to get used to being without him and they'll be missing him terribly."

When they said their bedtime prayers that night, they prayed for Lori and her family. Julie was so sad for her friend and could not fall asleep for a very long time.

It was November of 1969 and Mrs. Tyler had been talking to the class about the United States' space program. Everyone knew that a rocket spaceship called Apollo 11 had landed on the moon, and Neil Armstrong was the first man to walk on the moon, taking one small step for a man and a giant leap for mankind. It had happened in July while the kids were out of school for the summer and was big news in every household. Millions of people across the world watched a grainy black and white television broadcast of this historic event.

Now there was a second mission to the moon, Apollo 12. On the 19th of November, Mrs. Tyler rolled a television into the classroom on a cart with wheels. She announced that they were going to witness history today. The students were so excited to be watching history on TV and to have no school lesson!

"Children, in an orderly fashion, come to the front of the classroom and find a seat on the floor." There was a lot of whispering as they gathered around the television and Mrs. Tyler tuned in the station. The three buddies, Cathy, Lori and Julie, sat next to each another.

Cathy leaned over and whispered to Julie, "I wonder if it's a full moon?"

"I guess so. They might fall off if it's just a sliver of the moon," answered Julie as they giggled.

"Quiet, girls," said Mrs. Tyler. "Time to pay attention, everyone. Astronauts Conrad and Bean will be exiting the module soon."

That night at the Nevel supper table the girls were anxious to talk about what they were able to watch that day.

"Whose turn is it to pray?" Betty asked.

Karen said, "Julie's."

Julie said, "Nu-uh, I prayed last night. It's your turn, Gail."

Gail nodded and said the blessing. Then the food was passed around the table.

Paul asked, "So how was your day, girls? Anything exciting happen?" He winked at Betty; he had already been informed of the excitement from school and the probable topic for the evening.

Bonnie, Gail and Julie all started to talk at once. The room exploded in happy, jubilant chatter.

"Wait, wait, wait," Paul interrupted. "One at a time. It appears that you were all in the same classroom today."

Bonnie jumped in immediately, "Well in a sense, yes I guess we were. I think the whole school watched the men walking on the moon."

"It was amazing to watch," Gail marveled. "Like it was just a movie and not real. But it was real."

"Did you know that after they launched from Florida, the spaceship was hit by lightning?" Bonnie added. "But it didn't hurt anything too much."

Gail chimed in with, "The astronauts took a camera with them that would show us everything in color for the first time, but Mr. Bean broke it because he pointed it at the sun. That's what they said anyway and we could only see black and white even though it was a color TV."

"Imagine taking a color camera with you all the way to the moon and breaking it," said Paul. "Bet he felt bad. But then again, how bad can you feel when the whole world is watching you walk on the moon?"

Little Karen listened intently then, after thinking about it, wondered, "If we look at the moon tonight, will we see them?"

They all laughed and Betty said, "No, honey, they're too far away."

That confused Karen. "Then why do you always say look at the man on the moon?"

"That's the man in the moon, not on the moon…," Bonnie tried to explain. "Meaning you can see a man's face if you look at the moon just right." She could see Karen was even more confused than before.

Betty started singing, "I see the moon and the moon sees me. And the moon sees the one that I long to see."

Paul joined her, "So God bless the moon and God bless me. And God bless the one that I long to see." They finished in perfect harmony.

The girls applauded.

"Sing it again," Julie pleaded.

"But Mom, you always say no singing at the table," said Gail.

"They're the parents," Julie remarked in defense of Paul and Betty. "They can sing if they want."

Paul laughed, "That song came out in '53 when I was in Korea. It was one of our songs while we were separated. Even though we were so far apart, we knew we could both see the moon and were under the same sky. It's just that we had lots of space between us."

That night, the family went out on the porch after dark for a few minutes of moon-gazing.

Soon after the second moon landing was Thanksgiving, a favorite American holiday for the Nevels. The girls came home every day the week before and talked about what they learned in school about how Thanksgiving came to be. The younger ones drew turkeys onto construction paper by tracing around their hand prints and adding some of the bird's features. On Thanksgiving Day, Betty and Gram prepared a delicious turkey dinner with all of the trimmings. Paul went around the table and asked everyone what they were thankful for, then led in a special prayer of thanksgiving to God for all of His blessings and the freedom they enjoyed living in the United States of America.

Christmas that year was celebrated with great fanfare and traditions, as usual. Life on Asbury Lane continued to be filled with special moments and the making of memories.

TWENTY-THREE

Even before they moved to the farm on Asbury Lane, Paul had been thinking about where to build the new house he promised his wife. He would walk the perimeter of the land with his brother Jake and talk about possibilities. Paul had pictured extending the lane up the hill a bit from the other two houses. He also had the contractor for whom he worked take a look and they had to test for water where he anticipated drilling the well.

The decision was made on the ideal spot, the plans drawn up and everything was in place.

It was an exciting time as the day drew closer for construction to begin. Paul determined that March would be the best time to start, as soon as most of the winter snows had made their exit and the ground had thawed. He told the girls, "Every well-built house starts with a good foundation. You remember that as you get older."

Finally, crews arrived and dug a large hole for the basement and foundation. When all was in place, the cement truck rumbled in to pour the footer.

The entire family was to play a part in building the house and Julie was especially excited about helping. She liked to work beside her dad and learn to do things like placing a nail just right and using a hammer to pound it into a two-by-four or the dry wall. She loved how her father would use his fold-out measuring stick then quickly snap it back into place. Sometimes when he was measuring, he would let her hold a tool he used called a level and move it around until the little liquid bubble was right in the middle, confirming the boards or drywall were straight and level. "We don't want a crooked house now, do we? Every little detail is so important. No cheating or cutting corners when I'm on the job."

Paul wore a nail apron around his waist that had pockets for a hammer and nails. Julie decided she needed one, too. So Paul assigned an extra one he had to be her very own.

Often during the building process, Betty took her camera up the hill to take a few pictures of the progress.

"Now that's a picture." she said one day when she saw Julie in her shorts, T-shirt, cowboy boots and her own nail apron wrapped around her little waist. "Say cheese."

Julie struck a pose and her mother captured it for posterity.

Paul knew his kind of farming would never bring in much income and that he would always have to work another job. As much as he loved carpentry and would continue to use his skills on the side, he needed to find employment that would be steady regardless of the weather and provide the funds needed to take care of his family of six plus the farm, plus the new house he was building.

He heard that the local plant for PPG Industries, Pittsburgh Plate Glass, was hiring. He applied and was told the job was his if he could work swing shift. He was trained to do various jobs in the plant which made automotive car glass, often working in the screening room where they would test the glass before it was used in a vehicle. He put in long days of tedious work, often physically demanding. When the guys he worked with heard that he was a farmer, they asked what he was raising. His answer was, "Girls! Four daughters to be exact." It was a stressful time for Paul to start a new job in the middle of constructing his own house. But he was able to keep on schedule for the most part and Betty was glad that the extra carpentry work he was doing now was on their own house, which kept him close to home.

One day after the roof was on and Julie was pounding nails, it started to rain outside.

"Dad, if a bad storm comes with wind and rain, our new house will be okay, right? It won't fall down or anything, will it?"

"Yes, Julie, of course. That's why we're being real careful to build it right and make it strong so it will be a safe place for us to live in."

"You're a wise man, Dad."

Paul was amused by the comment. "Oh?" he inquired. "And what makes you say that?"

"Well in Sunday School, Teacher Ruth taught us a song about something

Jesus said." She began to sing. "The wise man built his house upon the rock, the wise man built his house upon the rock. The wise man built his house upon the rock, and the rains came tumbling down."

Her father had to chuckle and joined her in singing and doing the hand motions to the song. "The rains came down and the floods came up. The rains came down and the floods came up. The rains came down and the floods came up, and the house on the rock stood firm."

Paul applauded Julie's song and she smiled from ear to ear. That night after the girls were tucked into bed, Paul told Betty about Julie connecting the dots. "You know, sometimes it seems like what we say to the kids or what we hope they're learning goes in one ear and out the other. But every once in a while, something sticks. I love it when that happens."

Once the frame of the house was up, and Paul and his helpers were working on other details, it became a favorite place for the girls and their friends to play. They were warned to stay away from the stairs, but otherwise they could play house in the rooms that were framed but without walls, as long as they were careful and picked up after themselves when they were done.

Fortunately, Paul was not alone. Jake often came after work to help his big brother. And there were others. Don Focht, a friend and co-worker of Paul's who lived farther out the lane, lent his expertise quite often. His father had been the Nevels' milkman since they moved to the farm. In those days, many people outside of town had their milk delivered a couple times a week and placed in a milk box. Paul and Betty's milk box was an insulated silver metal square box that sat outside the door. Payment was left inside the box on the honor system.

Jim Harding, who had helped Paul find the farm, was now a plumber. After he married Judy, they rented their apartment from a man who had a plumbing business. He talked to his landlord about the benefits of learning the trade and decided to do it. He told Paul whenever he was ready to plumb the house, just to let him know and he would lend a hand. Paul and Jim often traded favors using their areas of expertise, not ever keeping score, but happy to help each other out. The Harding clan was one of the families who often spent Sunday afternoons at the farm. Daughter Pennie and Julie were friends from the time they shared cribs and toys in the church nursery, and son Troy came along after Karen. While Jim worked on plumbing details,

Judy would visit with Betty as the toddlers amused themselves and Pennie would join the girls playing house in the house.

It was not long before the drywall went up and the intriguing framework that lent itself to a make-believe world became enclosed and looked more like a house.

Buck pitched in with the house where he could, but had not been able to work regularly as a painter for some time after an illness that seemed to come and go. He had suffered from blood circulation problems since he could remember and developing frostbite on a few occasions from working in the cold weather had not helped his health. In fact, it had even hampered his ability to serve in the Army in his younger days. In 1944 during World War II, he was drafted into the Army and trained for three months at Fort Indiantown Gap, Pennsylvania, just a few hours from Altoona. The close proximity allowed Buck to return home on weekends, much to the delight of his wife and two girls. Young Betty and Marlene were always excited to see him and loved when he brought each of them a big Tootsie Roll or some sort of small gift. To the relief of his family, and before he was to be deployed, he was honorably discharged due to his condition, diagnosed as Raynaud's disease.

In December, two weeks before Christmas, Paul presented his promised gift to his bride and the Nevel family moved into the new house which instantly became a home. It was a warm and welcoming place to be, no matter the weather outside.

A cement sidewalk went from the driveway to three stair steps leading up to the left of the inviting front porch. When they poured the cement for the sidewalk, Paul had each of the four girls make a footprint, side by side, in the wet cement. Betty thought it was a genius idea and the girls had all kinds of fun being allowed to step in what felt like mud between their toes. They forever after used it to measure their growth and compare their foot sizes with themselves and with their friends.

The porch had a red brick backing, accentuated with two white, round, stately porch columns and a roof. It was flanked by white siding and four windows facing front on each side of the porch, two on the ground floor and two on the second floor. In the days when both Paul and Betty were growing up living in town, before there were televisions with many stations and other such distractions, the front porch was the hub of social life. Therefore, having a front porch with enough room for a couple of chairs was a given. This is also where they would proudly hang an American flag from a flag pole wall mount, and the milk box would be a fixture. Walking in the front door from the porch and entering the split level, one staircase led up and one led down.

The basement would be the last part of the house to be finished in the coming few years. The plan was for it to someday be a recreation room, or "rec room," with extra space for play and for guests. A Ben Franklin Stove was already in place in the basement and connected to the chimney. Designed to produce less smoke and more heat than an ordinary open fireplace, burning wood from their own woods would help to heat the house and allow them to save on using the electric floorboard heaters. Doors from the basement opened into the one-car garage and the mudroom, which included a laundry room and a small bathroom. There was an outside door on the side of the house by the driveway which opened into the mudroom, where Betty would make sure that shoes and boots came off, and the mud stayed!

From the small foyer inside the front door, the stairs going up, which were still bare wood and would be carpeted eventually, led to the living room to the right, and a hallway to three bedrooms and a full bath to the left. They wanted the living room to be comfortable, cozy and welcoming. Continuing straight from the stairway was the entrance into the kitchen, with plenty of counter and cabinet space for Betty and room for a kitchen table that seated six plus. Another open doorway led out of the kitchen to the dining room and a big picture window facing the woods. They agreed that outside that window would be a good place to put a bird feeder after they planted some trees in the yard. Betty's parents had a bird bath in their yard and she and her mom had always enjoyed birdwatching and trying to identify the birds they saw by looking them up in the World Book Encyclopedias. There was a back door to the house in the kitchen, with plans to have a patio out back one day. Betty envisioned picnic tables out there where they could enjoy meals outdoors on nice, warm days.

Paul was confident that his loving wife and wonderful mother to their children would make the house he built on Asbury Lane a home. And for Betty, the house was a constant reminder for her to count her blessings from God for giving her a man who worked hard, loved his family, dreamed big dreams and kept his promises.

The first Christmas in the new house was celebrated with fun family traditions, and more excitement than ever. There was no time to set up a large train platform, but Paul still managed to get his Sante Fe O-Gauge running a loop around the plump Christmas tree which they had cut down in the woods just the week before. The Christmas Eve caroling, opening stockings at Gram and Pap Pap's, Christmas morning program by the kids and opening of gifts was enjoyed by all. Betty and her mother prepared a scrumptious Christmas dinner and Buck tried to tease the kids into believing they were eating the turkey they'd seen in the yard the previous week, the one that got away at Thanksgiving.

Afternoon naps on the living room couch and chairs were in order for the adults as the kids played with their new toys. A light snow was falling outside, the wood in the Franklin Stove crackled as it sent its heat up the stairs, and the lights on the tree added a warm glow to the atmosphere. Paul's eyes were heavy as he stared for a few moments at the beautiful ceramic Nativity set his mother-in-law had made that was sitting on an end table, and relished a rare moment of relaxation. With Betty leaning back against him on the couch, hearing Silent Night playing on the hi-fi stereo record player, he whispered a prayer of thanks as he drifted off to the lyrics, "Sleep in heavenly peace, sleep in heavenly peace."

With the evening came visitors with season's greetings to share their joy, not to mention their Christmas cookies that Betty had somehow still managed to make in the midst of the move.

❧

After a cold, snowy winter, spring came to the farm at last, a thing of beauty as the fields and woods burst with life in pastel colors and sweet aromas of blossoming trees and flowers. It passed all too quickly for Betty, but the girls were excited and ready for their summer break from school.

The annual field day was set aside at school for special activities and took place the end of May, just before classes were dismissed for the summer. Sometimes called "Track and Field Day," it was entirely dedicated to outdoor activities such as races, relays and games. There was something for everyone, and all of the kids as well as teachers looked forward to this special day.

Julie loved to run up and down the lane and on the playground. She could even outrun some of the boys, so she thought she might do pretty well in the field day competitions. However, five days before the races, one of the larger boys fell on her when they were playing on the monkey bars during recess. Julie told Mrs. Tyler her ankle hurt and the teacher sent her to the nurse who saw some swelling and promptly propped it up and put ice on it.

Later, after riding the usual route on the school bus to her stop, Julie stood and started to make her way down the high bus steps. Suddenly she cried out in pain. Her ankle had swollen even more and she almost fell down the steps. Gail came up behind her to help and a neighbor offered them a ride home, as it was clear that Julie would not be able to walk any distance.

Betty tended to Julie's ankle the same way the school nurse did with elevation and ice.

"Oww that ice is cold! Do we have to use ice, Mom?" she cried.

"Yes, we have to use ice," Betty replied patiently, but firmly. "It will make the swelling go down. Did the boy know he hurt you? Did you tell the teacher on recess duty?"

"I guess it was just an accident. I wanted to blame him and tell on him; I was so mad."

"But...you didn't?" Betty inquired.

"Well really he just lost his grip and fell and I happened to be under him. It was embarrassing. I said I was fine. I want to go to school this week because Friday is field day! Please let me go to school!" Julie pleaded.

Betty agreed to let her go, but only with an ace bandage around her ankle and with orders to be careful. She wrote a note to Mrs. Tyler asking her to make sure Julie's activities were limited.

The Bellwood-Antis staff and students had the good fortune of blue skies and sun for Field Day. Julie's ankle was getting better and she was determined to participate. The first grade girls lined up for the 50-yard dash.

Ready, set, Go! And they were off. Julie pulled ahead with a steady lead over the field. Pushing pain aside, she made her little legs go as fast as they could carry her. Just before the finish line, she saw a blur to her left. It was Cathy with flailing arms and a big smile as she passed Julie just in time to beat her at the tape. Cathy was very excited about her victory. Julie sulked.

It was an unfortunate ending to Field Day for one first grader.

TWENTY-FOUR

It was a cold Friday the 13th and Bonnie and Gail were off to a Sweethearts Banquet at church with the youth group. February on the farm in rural Pennsylvania was not exactly a month to plan events outside. Though the kids still braved the bitter cold to ride sleds and build snowmen, they were getting a little stir crazy from a long winter. The two oldest girls were looking forward to getting out of the house for a fun evening with their friends.

Betty thought the only nice part of February was the promise that March was just around the corner. It was not snowing and the roads were clear, so she told Paul she would drop the girls off at the church on her way to the hospital to visit her father. That allowed him to stay home with Julie and Karen. Buck had been hospitalized for over a week and his health was steadily declining. The doctors did not understand why his kidneys were shutting down. The family knew his condition was grave, however no one realized that he would not be getting better.

Julie and Karen were in their bedroom using their play kitchen and dishes to have their very own Sweethearts Banquet since they were not allowed to go with their big sisters. Paul was watching the CBS Evening News. It was the one television channel they could count on after running an antenna to the top of the hill, though NBC came in as well when it was not raining.

"Nothing new on the news," he thought, as Walter Cronkite covered yet another anti-Vietnam War protest denounced by President Nixon. Just as the anchor signed off with, "And that's the way it is, Friday, February 13th, 1970...," the phone rang. It was Betty calling from the hospital with a shaky voice, and some tragic news. Buck Myers had suddenly passed from this earth at the young age of sixty. Raynaud's disease turned out to be a blessing that kept him from fighting in the war, yet a curse that led to complications and renal failure bringing about a premature end to his life. Betty lost the second most important man in her life.

Paul tried to remain calm as he called to ask Mrs. Kutruff if she could watch the two girls. He needed to be by his wife's side. He did not want to say much to the little ones yet, worried that they were too young to understand. But while rushing to leave the house, Julie knew something was terribly wrong and finally mustered the courage to ask her dad why they were leaving so quickly in the middle of the evening. He stooped down at the bottom of the stairs, put her coat on her and answered as gently as he could, "Honey, Pap Pap went to heaven." He choked back the tears when he saw her bewildered little face and picked her up and held her closely. "It's going to be okay. Mommy and I need to go be with Gram, so Mrs. Kutruff will take care of you for a bit. We'll be back soon."

When Julie and Karen went into the neighbor's house, they were met by a sweet, caring Mrs. Kutruff, to whom Paul whispered a few things and then he was gone. The Kutruff grandkids were there and Karen jumped right into playing with them, but Julie sat somberly in a chair choking back tears and wondering how they could just go on playing with all this sadness around.

Paul stopped by the church to pick up the older girls. They were surprised to see him there earlier than they expected. "But Dad, the party's not over yet. We are still going to play another game and…"

He interrupted. "I'm sorry, girls. I have some sad, sad news."

Broken-hearted, they went to Gram's house to wait for Betty to bring her home. It was indeed a very sad, sad night for all of them.

The Myers and Nevel families and their friends gathered to mourn and celebrate a life well lived. Five years and one week following the death of Marlene, her father was taken from them. It seemed uncanny that they were both born in the month of April, and both passed in the month of February.

As difficult as February was, spring did eventually come, a refreshing season ushering in hope for better days ahead. Summer followed and joy was tangible again; the family was in their new house and Paul was looking forward to mowing the fields and bringing in a barn-full of hay. He was living his dream as a farmer and Betty had a new house better than anything she had even imagined. Gram spent a considerable amount of time with them; the country air on Asbury Lane and precious moments with her granddaughters were a balm for her mourning soul.

TWENTY-FIVE

While the girls were reveling in life on the farm, trouble was brewing.

She had had enough. "If they call me 'Snorky' one more time, I am outta here," sulked seven-year-old Julie.

Indeed, sometimes being the third child was not a fun branch on the family tree. Not only did she get the hand-me-downs and used toys, she was the target of the jokes by her older sisters.

Snorky was a character from a children's television show called *The Banana Splits Adventure Hour*. It was Hanna-Barbera Productions' first venture into mixing animation with live action. *The Banana Splits* was a fictional rock band composed of four funny animal characters: Fleegle, Bingo, Drooper, and Snorky. Sponsored by Kellogg's Cereals, they naturally had a cereal to correspond with the show and characters.

Snorky was the keyboard player. He was a poufy purple elephant with a long trunk and though he was cute, he only spoke in honking noises. Bonnie and Gail thought the name fit Julie, especially since she was often catching colds and making snorky kinds of noises.

One day, Betty noticed that the other girls were playing in the basement, but Julie was still in her room. She went to check on her and found her lying on her bed with a blanket pulled over her head.

"Why so gloomy, Julie?"

"Oh nothing, I'm just not feeling great 'cause of my cold," the little girl pouted.

"Well, resting is what you need then. I'll call you when it's time for supper."

"Mom?" Her mother waited sensing that something was on Julie's mind. "Sometimes I get mad when Bonnie and Gail call me names."

"Oh? Well they shouldn't be calling you names. What kind of names?"

"I don't want to tell you, but it's not nice."

From under the blanket, she heard Betty turn on her heels and head toward the basement. Julie's gloom lightened a little when she heard her mom reprimanding her big sisters. She could not hear all that was being said, but she felt vindicated. Regardless, she knew it was not over though, because next they would be calling her a tattletale.

When Betty went back to the kitchen after scolding the girls, they started to devise a plan of vengeance.

"I can't believe she told Mom. We're just teasing her! She can't take a joke," Bonnie whispered.

"Big old baby tattletale," responded Gail.

Not long after, Mom called the girls for supper and Dad was already there, hungry and in good spirits after a great day on the farm.

They sat down and Paul asked, "Whose turn is it?"

It was Betty's turn to pray. She tagged on a request that the Lord would help the girls to appreciate their sisters and all get along. It was quieter around the dinner table than usual.

After dinner, the older girls walked down to the barn with Paul while Betty had Julie and Karen help her clean up after dinner.

Karen, oblivious to the feud going on between her sisters, wanted Julie to go outside and play. "No, honey, Julie needs to stay in this evening; she's not feeling well."

"But Mom," complained Julie, "I'm not that sick."

"You have a cold and you said this morning your throat hurt again. You need to just rest this evening, no running around outside."

Meanwhile, Karen went out to the swing set by the apple tree beside the house. Betty could keep an eye on her from the window and knew she would swing until sundown. The littlest child loved the swing.

For Julie, she was confined to the couch.

Betty unfolded the orange and yellow crocheted afghan, one of Gram's works of art, which was draped over the back of the sofa and tucked it in around Julie. "How about I turn on some cartoons for you?" She felt her forehead. "Well you don't feel like you have a fever, maybe it's just a case of the sniffles."

In Julie's ears it might as well have been "a case of the snorkels" as she blew her nose and put on her best pout face.

Betty crossed the room and turned on the TV.

"Don't put on that *Banana Splits* cartoon, Mom."

Betty was surprised. "I thought you liked that one?"

"Not anymore," sulked Julie.

With the horses fed, Bonnie and Gail asked if they could stay in the barn for a while and groom them. "Okay," their dad answered. "Just be careful and you know not to stand behind the horses where they can't see you."

When Paul left to check on the fence where a deer had run through the day before, the girls vetted their anger as they brushed down Dusty and White Socks.

"I still can't believe she told Mom. She just wanted to get us in trouble," complained Bonnie.

"Maybe it's 'cause she's sick and just wants the attention," suggested Gail.

By the time everyone was in the house for the evening, it was time to wash up, brush teeth, put pajamas on and say their bedtime prayers. Bonnie and Gail shared the back bedroom, with the full size white canopy bed. Julie and Karen had the smaller bedroom and slept in bunkbeds.

"Are you sad?" Karen asked.

"Yeah, kinda. Bonnie and Gail don't like me," said Julie climbing up the ladder to the top bunk.

"Oh yes they do, Julie, you're their sister."

But Julie knew her younger sister did not understand her plight. As she saw it, Karen was the baby and got everything she wanted, including all the attention. Bonnie and Gail would never dare pick on her.

"Well, they're mean to me sometimes."

There was a tap on the door and it creaked open a bit. "Can we come in?" Bonnie and Gail asked as they gingerly walked into the room.

"No, you can't," snipped Julie.

But they entered anyway and gave Karen a goodnight hug and kiss then blew kisses to Julie on the top bunk.

"Sorry about earlier," Bonnie said. "We were just joking around. We didn't expect you to get upset."

"Besides," Gail added with a giggle, "You're a cute...Snorky!"

As they ran out, Julie threw her pillow at them but it was too late and just hit the door. Karen was amused but Julie was not. She pulled the covers over her head, fumed and schemed on how she would get them back before she drifted off to sleep.

The next morning after breakfast when everyone was off to do their own thing, Julie slipped into her bedroom, shut the door and started to pack some of her belongings in her knapsack. She took her pocketknife, canteen, a change of clothes, notepad and pencil. It was time for her to step out on her own. She was running away.

Their dad had helped the girls erect a two-man green canvas tent in the field below the house the week before. Julie figured she could at least escape to it and no one would find her for a long, long time. That would show them that she was no Snorky.

When it looked as if the coast was clear, she hurried out of the house and down the road. Slipping into the tent, she set up house. She heard her father come up the lane from the barn and there were sounds of others out and about doing various things. After some time went by, she took out her pencil and paper and started to write.

"Dear Diary, today is the day I am taking a stand and starting out on my own..."

She wrote a little more, until the emotion from her break for freedom caused her to become sleepy. She laid down wondering when someone would miss her or if they even would, ever. Then she then dozed off to sleep.

After coming back to the house when his chores were finished, Paul settled down to read the newspaper when Betty called up from the basement, "Honey, have you seen Julie?"

"No, did you lose her?" he joked.

"I thought maybe she went to the barn with you, because she's not in her bed. And she's not out with Karen on the swing."

"Did you check Bonnie and Gail's room?"

"I doubt they would've let her in, but I'll check." Betty tapped on the door to Bonnie and Gail's room, "Girls, is Julie in there?"

"No way," snapped Gail, but then she realized that was the kind of attitude that would get her in trouble. She changed her tone to a sweeter, gentler one, "I mean...no, she is not, Mom."

Betty was starting to wonder if Julie was playing a trick on them. She hoped she had not wandered off by herself; she knew better.

Meanwhile, back in the tent, Julie woke with a start and it took her a moment to realize where she was. It was getting warm inside that canvas as the sun climbed higher in the sky. She rubbed her sleepy eyes and reached into her knapsack for a Kleenex to wipe her dripping nose. It just made her think of Snorky and she remembered why she had left home. "I hope they never find me," she thought, "but I do hope they notice eventually that I'm gone. If they don't find me by tonight, maybe Mom will find the note on my pillow."

Just then she heard the front door of the house closing and heard her mother calling for her. The voices of her sisters joined in. She could tell they were going around the house, over by the shed in the yard and behind the wood pile.

She was at least gratified that they had missed her.

Footsteps on the gravel going down the lane told her that someone was going to look for her in the barn; however, she hoped they would not think to look for her in the tent.

Searching the immediate grounds around the house and the barn did not turn up the little girl so, the search party reconvened in the house. Suspicion on Betty's part fell on the other two, "Did you make up with Julie last night like I asked you to? Do you know where she is, because if you do, you had better tell me, now?"

"She was upset last night," said Karen. "She said her sisters don't like her."

Instantly, Bonnie and Gail looked at each other, wondering if they should reveal to their mom the last words they said to Julie.

"We tried to make up…," Bonnie started to say.

"You called her Snorky," Karen chimed in.

Now Karen was the tattle tale.

"Maybe we should search her bedroom and see if anything is missing," Bonnie offered quickly and headed toward the younger girls' room before her mother could respond.

They immediately noticed that Julie's diary was gone. She always kept it on the top of her dresser. Betty opened the closet. No knapsack on the hook.

Gail climbed the ladder then she blurted out, "There's a note! She left a note on her pillow."

She was going to read it when her mother snatched it away from her.

"I know I'm not wanted around here, so I am running away. Love, Julie," Betty read out loud.

"Oh dear," sighed Betty. "Wherever could she have gone?"

"Maybe she's lost in the woods," offered Bonnie.

"Uh oh, she could have been eaten by lions or tigers or bears," suggested Gail.

"Oh no!" Bonnie finished for her.

"Lions and tigers?" Karen was alarmed.

"There are no lions or tigers in our woods," Betty reassured the youngest. Then her glance and shushing hand motion told Gail and Bonnie that they were not to bring up the bear that had recently smashed the neighbor's bird feeder or they would be in even more trouble than they already were.

"Don't worry, Mom, she'll get tired or scared or hungry and come home soon," Bonnie said.

Gail thought that was funny and giggled which made Bonnie giggle and even Karen got the giggles.

"Girls, that is not funny. She must feel pretty hurt about something to do this and she's been sick. I don't like not knowing where she is."

"What about the tent?" asked Paul from the doorway. "She loves playing in there. I don't think she'd try to get to the tree house on her own."

Gail ran out the door with Bonnie close behind and Karen on their heels. They ran down the hill, into the field and to the tent. "Julie. Julie, are you in there?"

Gail knelt down to unzip the flap door.

Rats! Julie was not happy that she was found, but she was cornered now.

"Julie!" exclaimed Bonnie. "If you're in there, Mom is starting to get really worried. Come out of there now."

Betty was hurrying down the hill as Julie crawled from the tent. She reached down to hug her. "Thank goodness, you're okay. What were you thinking?"

"I told you, Mom. I told you they were calling me names. And you are always busy looking after Karen, and I just didn't think anyone would notice if I was gone."

"Wouldn't notice? Julie, don't be silly. We love you, and you are just as important as anyone else in this family." She kissed her daughter then glared at the two older ones. "And there will be no more name-calling."

For their part, Bonnie and Gail made every effort to appear contrite.

"Don't you ever do something like that again, Julie," Betty continued. "You scared us."

As they walked back to the house, Julie thought to herself that, sometimes the third child just had to run away from home to get noticed.

For a while, after the running away incident, Julie's older sisters tried to be a little nicer to her.

Her persistent cold and sore throat worsened over the next couple days and when she ran a fever, her mother took her to see the doctor. Tests revealed that Julie had strep throat - again. This was the fourth time in a few months. It was always a fight to persuade Julie to take her medicine, as she could not swallow the large pills. Betty tried to get her to take the penicillin by breaking the pills in half or crushing them up in jelly on her toast or in a spoonful of sugar. She figured if it worked for Mary Poppins, maybe it would work for her. It seemed that as soon as Julie was done with the penicillin, the strep would return.

The doctor blamed her tonsils and advised them to have the culprits removed.

The result was that Julie was in the hospital for three days and had a tender throat for several weeks, but the cure was plenty of ice cream, Jello and extremely soft foods. In her own way, she subtly flaunted her fortune over her sisters. Oh, and a lot of attention from Mom and Dad, and Gram. Not bad for the third of four kids.

TWENTY-SIX

Music continued to be an important part of the Nevel household. Paul, with his beautiful baritone voice, had sung in church and school choirs from a young age and played clarinet in the high school band. He and Glenn had formed "The Sterling Gospel Quartet" with Glenn's brother George, and Paul and Glenn's Uncle Pete, another one of the Rudasill fifteen. The quartet sang for many years for church services and events and around town here, there and everywhere.

Sunday evenings were a favorite of the folks at the First Church of Christ on 6th Avenue and 9th Street. Uncle Pete would lead the congregational singing by taking favorites from the hymnal, accompanied by the majestic pipe organ. This was commonly called a "Singspiration." The youth group traditionally sat together in their usual couple of pews and called out their favorite page numbers they had memorized, which were sure to be the livelier hymns. Uncle Pete also played the harmonica, or as he called it, the mouth organ, and it was always a delight to those in attendance.

Paul was a favorite soloist for the weddings of their church friends and families. Betty still picked up the accordion from time to time and delighted in singing alto in the choir along with Paul. After they were married, they continued to play their instruments for Sunday school class parties and various programs at church.

They made the joint decision that their children would take piano lessons since the piano was a good base instrument on which to start. Bonnie and Gail began piano lessons at seven years of age. Before it was even Julie's turn to begin, she would sit at the piano and mimic her sisters and could not wait to take her own lessons. The instructor who taught her sisters was no longer teaching, so Betty found a new piano teacher who lived in Homer's Gap, which was not far from the farm. Her name was Carolyn Snow. Julie liked Mrs. Snow from the beginning and caught on quickly using her sisters' beginner piano books by John Thompson. Of course Betty had to keep on the girls to mind their practice times and not cut them short, but once they were able to play music they enjoyed, it was no longer much of an issue.

Life around Asbury Lane was always filled with delights and new experiences.

There were lots of wild barn cats and a few tame ones that Paul allowed to stay to keep the mice population under control. The Nevel kids and their friends loved to go hunting for new baby kittens in the hayloft. Paul knew when a mother cat was about to give birth and would tip them off so they could search for them. They would choose their favorites, name them and claim them as their own. If they spent enough time with them, the cats would grow up fairly tame. Over time, Bonnie and Gail talked their mother into keeping one of the kittens as an indoor pet. She was an adorable, furry gray clumsy kitten with white markings and they named her Fluffy. Over the years, Betty was never one to allow pets in her house, any house, so this was an exception. The girls were overjoyed and took good care of Fluffy. She still loved to go outside though, to visit her family in the barn and roam the fields. And she did not forget her job as mouse hunter. Apparently, she knew it was her responsibility because she occasionally brought one of her catches around to show off.

One Saturday afternoon a young man named Lynn came to the farm to hunt. He and his family were friends of the Nevels' from church. Paul was never much of a hunter himself, but he allowed responsible hunters whom he trusted to hunt on his property. He especially did not mind the hunters shooting ground hogs, which were a constant nuisance, digging large holes in his hay fields.

As Lynn's story was recounted later, he came out of the woods into a clearing and whistled as one would to catch a ground hog's attention. The sound would usually cause them to stand upright and look around, presenting the hunter a perfect shot. He saw something rise up and he took the shot. Only it was not a ground hog this time. When he walked closer to the target he had hit, he realized it was a cat. At first he felt badly, but knew it probably was not a big deal since there were plenty of wild barn cats everywhere. Nevertheless, he told Paul about it and Paul also assumed it was one of the wild felines.

That evening, when the girls were getting ready to go in for the night, they were concerned because they could not find Fluffy. She would usually come to the door in the evening and meow to be let in, but there was no sign of her.

"Can I look in the barn, Mom?" Bonnie asked.

"Okay, but hurry. It's almost your bedtime."

Bonnie came back disappointed. "Didn't find her. I hope she didn't wander off and get lost."

When there was still no sign of Fluffy by the next evening, Paul began to have an uneasy feeling about the cat that Lynn shot. He took a walk to the area where the hunter had been and, sure enough, sadly enough, found gray fur among the remains.

The love of God may demand forgiveness. Regardless, it would be a very long time until the Nevel girls spoke to Lynn again. Cats may come and cats may go, but there will never be another Fluffy.

TWENTY-SEVEN

In the field below and to the right of the house, Paul had parked the old '52 red Ford pickup truck that Mr. Kutruff had left behind, which was on its last legs, or wheels. He sometimes used it to run around the farm, but it was beyond passing a state inspection and the odds of it making it very far beyond Asbury Lane were not good. It finally gave up the ghost, so to speak, and sat rusting away, tires worn and flat, an eye sore in Betty's estimation.

She finally spoke up. "Honey, when are you going to get rid of that old piece of junk? It looks terrible sitting there with hay growing up through the floorboards. I know the kids like to play in it, but one of these days they're going to open the door and find a snake to greet them," Betty persisted.

"You're probably right on that," grinned Paul. "But I'm sure we'll hear the screams."

"Not funny, Paul."

"It's just not the easiest thing to move, dear. It won't run and the only way I can tow it would be with the tractor. I don't want to make headlines in the Mirror." He motioned in the air as though pointing to the headline story. "Farmer tows junk truck with tractor down Route 220, turns heads and holds up traffic."

In the meantime, Julie and her playmates were glad it was not going anywhere. They had a whole Bonnie and Clyde adventure going on surrounding that truck and they needed it for their getaway car. Julie usually played the role of Bonnie, David was Clyde and any others who came along were assigned roles as criminal accomplices or cops. They would make a heist from the local bank, faces half covered with Paul's old handkerchiefs, donning hats and sunglasses and armed with squirt guns and cap guns. They made a narrow escape and drove off in the snazzy sports get-away car, formerly known as the old junk '52 Ford pickup truck, taking turns behind the big metal steering wheel, pushing all the buttons on the dash to shoot guns and give them turbo speed.

Sunday afternoon had rolled around again and it was the perfect spring day for an adventure. After church and following Betty's traditional Sunday roast beef meal, Julie donned her play clothes and cowboy boots, gathered some supplies and went outside to wait for her cousins.

Glenn and his family were the first to arrive. David also wore his cowboy boots and brought a couple of bandanas and his cap gun. Jake and Mary were next with their kids in tow. Patty, David and Julie talked about what they wanted to play. David's older sister Joyce went inside the house to find Gail and Bonnie, as did Patty's older sister Debbie when they showed up. Patty's brother Marvin felt a little left out when Aunt Susie's boys did not come, being the only older boy among the cousins, but he liked to help his father and Uncle Paul with whatever projects they had to do around the farm. Otherwise, pestering the girls was kind of fun.

"I'll be Bonnie, you be Clyde," Julie said to David. "Who do you want to be, Patty?"

"I'll be the police trying to catch you, if I can be Bonnie next."

"Okay. Let's make the garage the bank, and wait 'til you see what I got." Julie opened a small brown paper lunch bag to reveal a stack of money.

A collective "Wow!" came from the other two.

An adventure ensued, with Clyde robbing the bank of all its money at gunpoint and the cop running after him. His accomplice Bonnie had the get-away car revved up and ready a block away. Clyde managed to outrun the cop to the car and off they went, tires screeching, pointing and shooting their guns out the windows. At last the cop fell, exhausted from the chase, and called for backup.

While the robbery was taking place, the older siblings were chatting about school the past week and deciding what to do with their afternoon. Joyce loved visiting the farm and was not enthused about the prospect of being stuck inside all day. "It's so nice out, let's go for a walk."

"Let's play a game first," Debbie suggested. "Then we can go for a walk after that."

"Monopoly," said Bonnie. It was one of their favorites. She brought it to the table and opened the box. "Wait, something is missing…Where is the money? There's no money in here."

Immediately, Debbie suspected her brother was playing a trick on them. "Marvin. What did you do with the Monopoly money?"

Marvin, unsure of why he was being accused, looked around in confusion. "I don't know anything about any money. I promise!"

They were all suspicious of each other thinking one of them was playing a joke, when suddenly they heard the sound of popping cap guns outside and the fleeing Bonnie and Clyde. The unsuspecting cop found her backup, without even expecting it, when the older kids ran from the house and were hot on Bonnie and Clyde's trail. Unfortunately for the bank robbers, they were unable to escape in the car and their ill-gotten gain was taken from them.

TWENTY-EIGHT

There was always something to do at Asbury Lane and on Sundays it was an exciting place for young kids. The anticipation usually started in church.

When Julie and Pennie had been reprimanded by their parents for whispering back and forth in church, they resorted to passing notes.

"Are you coming out to the farm today?" Julie scribbled.

"Hope so. Will beg dad," Pennie wrote back.

"Bring clothes for the woods. We'll go to the tree house," responded Julie.

Pennie was writing back when she felt a firm tap on her shoulder from behind. Both girls heard a familiar and distinct clearing of the throat and felt the heat rising to their faces as they quickly straightened up and sat at attention. No one wanted to face the wrath of Mrs. Turner.

She was a staunchly righteous woman who wore her gray hair up in a bun and her rhinestone cat eye glasses at the end of her nose. She loved the Lord almost as much as she loved the Ten Commandments and her mission in life was to make sure everyone else did too. The First Church of Christ was a community and the first rule of the community was that every kid was expected to respect and obey every adult member of the church. When Mrs. Turner spoke, or rather cleared her throat, the girls were obligated to obey her unspoken decree: pay attention.

As soon as the last note of the closing song "The Family of God" was sung, the girls bolted out of their pew to avoid facing the stern-faced woman. As they hurried out, Julie said, "See you in a while crocodile."

"See you later, alligator," Pennie replied and they were off to find their parents.

Jim and Judy had already decided to go to the farm that afternoon, so Pennie did not have to beg, after all. Glenn and Peggy were going too, as were Jake and Mary.

Julie was always thrilled to have as many of her friends and cousins there who could come. Her motto was "the more, the merrier."

Once everyone was at Asbury Lane, Julie's gang wasted no time in preparing for the day's adventure. They packed canteens and apples then set off. Their usual route to the woods was to walk down the lane to the barn and take a left where the lane went right. Continuing straight ahead, they passed the shed for the hay bailer, went through the hay field and to the entrance to the woods. As they walked into the shade of the woods, there was a fork in the trail. Taking a right led to a nice, wide open path that gradually ascended until it opened into a field at the top of the hill. Paul could drive his tractor through the open space and it was a good trail for riding horses. Going left at the fork led to more rugged terrain where the path had at one time been a creek bed and was uneven with lots of rocks. After most rains, it was muddy and little pools of water would form and provide a playground for frogs and water insects, sometimes even crayfish. The trail was also ascending and would eventually lead to some pretty steep hills with a clearing beyond where the power lines cut through the area.

The tree house, as the kids referred to it, was on the creek bed route about half a mile up and a little off to the left of the beaten path. It was in a big oak tree whose branches reached far and wide, some hanging over another creek. No one knew who had built the original tree house, which now lay in ruins, just a few boards nailed to the tree. Someone had built a ladder out of tree branches and used it as a tree stand for hunting deer. There was a perfect half circle of a clearing around the tree, carpeted with soft green moss. The creek on the other side of the tree was down in a gully, like a moat to an enchanted castle. In Julie's imagination this was a mini fortress, a secret hideout that needed to be guarded and protected by her and her friends.

This particular Sunday, they would work on improving the grounds. David and Pennie took on the campfire area. Julie and Patty gathered fallen branches and stones to pile up as a border around the perimeter. After working for an hour or so, it was time for a break. Julie slid down the bank of the moat to the creek and filled up their aluminum canteens with cold spring water. She let the bubbling brook flow into each of them, put the lid on and then tossed them up to David one by one. He gave her a hand as she crawled back up the bank. They sat down on the moss around the circle of stones that enclosed the campfire pit.

"My dad says we shouldn't do this," Patty announced.

"What?" asked Pennie.

"Drink water out of the creek. There could be a dead animal in it or something and we could get sick or even poisoned."

"I drink out of the creek all the time and never get sick, but suit yourselves," Julie replied rather curtly then guzzled from her canteen. They all followed suit. Patty was hesitant, but did not want to be left out. Kid peer pressure was the rule of the day.

They each had an apple and some pretzels that Julie had brought in her backpack.

"It's looking good around here," David remarked. "What else do we need to do?" He stood up and started toward the tree. "We should bring some nails next time and…"

Suddenly he doubled over and began to moan. Then he fell to the ground, holding his stomach and rolling back and forth in pain. The others jumped up and gathered around him, distraught.

"Oh no. What's wrong David? What can we do?" Julie looked at Pennie and said, "Should one of us run back to the house and get an adult?"

Just then David stopped moaning as his eyes closed and he went limp.

Patty screamed, "David!? Wake up! Oh, it was the water. I told you we shouldn't drink it!"

Then Patty began to cry while Julie was trying to keep her wits about her.

"Grab your canteen, Pennie. Maybe if we sprinkle water on his face, it will help him come to."

Pennie did just that and David's hands went to his face and his body started to shake. The girls were even more frightened now.

"Maybe he's having a seizure. I'm gonna run to get someone," said Julie.

Kneeling, Pennie tried to dab some more water on his face. She was leaning over him, "David, David, can you hear me?" But his body shook even more.

Just as Julie was about to run, he started making high pitched sounds, muffled by his hands covering his face. The girls were trying not to panic. However, it was just too funny and David could no longer contain it. He burst out in laughter.

"What??" Pennie glared at him angrily.

"You're okay? Is this…wait, were you joking?" asked Julie.

Patty wiped her tears as the truth dawned on her and she just wanted to kick him.

So amused by the results of his practical joke, David rolled on the ground still laughing.

Not so amused, Pennie followed through on her impulse to douse him with water and really dosed him good this time with the water in her canteen.

"Hey, no fair," yelped David.

"Yes, fair," cried Pennie as she emptied the bottle over him.

He jumped up and ran, still chuckling that he pulled one over on the girls. They ran after him with shouts of, "Wait 'til I get my hands on you!" and "You are in big trouble, boy, you are in for it!"

When Julie finally caught up with David, she grabbed the back of his shirt to slow him down and stop him.

"That was just plain mean, David," she scolded him. "You scared us. And guess what else?"

David was out of breath, but still had a grin on his face. "What?"

"You're it," she said as she slapped his arm and ran off. A game of tag was underway, with the big oak tree for home base.

Another hour of play went by, then they heard the bell. Betty kept a dinner bell on a shelf Paul had built into the wall over the sink in the kitchen. She always liked bells and had a small collection of decorative ones. Most of them had little clappers that were not loud enough to be heard from very far way. There was one bell, however, that she kept for calling the kids and sometimes Paul back to the house. When they heard that bell ringing, they knew not to question it and not to delay, but to get home as quickly as possible.

"Time to go, guys." Julie announced.

"Rats," said Pennie.

"Let's take the shortcut through the field," said Julie. "C'mon I'll show you, follow me."

The kids gathered their things and started back down the trail. Before they had gone very far, Julie led them off the path and through the brush and trees. Patty complained when she was seemingly attacked by a sticker bush. The biggest obstacle when off the cleared pathway, was being stuck by jaggers, prickles and burrs. Pennie helped unstick her and they continued forging through until they came to a clearing. It was an open field, a pasture where the cows grazed.

When the Kutruffs owned the farm, it was a dairy farm. They raised milk cows and used the little house as a spring house to keep the milk cold before selling it to area businesses. One of the businesses to whom they proudly provided milk was Hershey's Chocolate Company. Milton Hershey started his business in the heart of eastern Pennsylvania farmland, well supplied with milk from area farmers.

After the Second World War, as the company grew and began to introduce new products, their need for more milk led them to expand their territory. Mr. Kutruff or one of the boys would drive a truck load of milk in glass bottles to a meeting place along the two-lane Route 220 and transfer the milk to the Hershey drivers. When the Kutruffs sold the farm to Paul and Betty, their son Bill took the milk cows to a farm he had purchased nearby. Paul was left with some dairy equipment in the barn, but he was more interested in riding horses than milking cows. A few years down the road, he began to buy two or three beef cattle each year to raise and have butchered. It was an economic way to provide healthy meat for his family.

The kids came upon the field where the beef cattle were grazing.

Julie warned the others, "There's a barbed wire fence and we just have to climb through. C'mon, it's easy, I've done it lots of times."

"But where are the cows?" asked Patty.

Julie shrugged her shoulders and went first to show them how. David was next. There were four strands of the fence evenly spaced out. Julie helped hold the middle two of them apart for him to squeeze through. Patty was next without any problem getting to the other side, breathing a sigh of relief.

Then she spotted them, "Oh there they are. And here they come!"

The cows had seen the activity over by the fence and, seemingly interested, they started slowly walking in the direction of the children.

Pennie was hesitant. "Uh, I don't know if I want to go this way. Can I go around?"

"No, c'mon Pen," Julie coaxed her. "It's too far to go around now and you might get lost. Mom rang the bell, remember? We have to hurry. You can do it."

"Okay," conceded Pennie, "Help me please."

Julie held the fence apart and Pennie leaned through without a scratch. "See, that wasn't so bad."

"Well I beat the fence but I don't know if I can beat...them." Pennie pointed back in the direction of the cattle.

Julie glanced over and saw that apparently the cows' curiosity had been peaked and they were running toward the kids. David and Patty were already halfway across the field; they had not waited when they saw the animals were picking up their pace.

Julie was confident, "Don't worry, they won't hurt us."

"Let's not take any chances!" Pennie called out and took off running faster than she had ever run in her life.

The other two were already through the fence on the other side of the field and were not far from the house. Julie was a fast runner, but this time Pennie won the race. The cows were closing in as the girls approached the next fence. Julie ducked under the wire but was distracted when the bell rang again. Just then she heard Pennie screaming and turned around to see her halfway through the fence, surrounded by a whole lot of beef. The back of her shirt had snagged on the barbed wire as she attempted to crawl through and in Pennie's terrified mind she only had moments left to live before she was trampled and eaten by cows! Before Julie could unsnag the shirt, Pennie in her panic pulled hard enough that her shirt ripped and she made a narrow escape. She sat on the ground trying to catch her breath, her heart pounding and her knees weak. She wasn't sure if she wanted to laugh from relief or to cry.

Julie, who had been certain of Pennie's survival all along, was trying not to laugh. But when one of the cows let out a bellowing "moo," they both broke into a fit of giggles.

By the time the four kids were safely at the house, Betty had supper ready for everyone.

"Where have you been?" demanded Betty. "We were starting to get worried."

"Goodness gracious, Pen, what happened to your shirt?" exclaimed Judy.

"Well, we took a short cut on the way back and I... I kind of got into a fight with a barbed wire fence." Julie and Pennie looked at each other and started to laugh again. "I'm okay though, because I found out I can outrun a cow."

They all gathered around the kitchen and Paul said a prayer thanking God for good friends and good food. Betty served as the hostess and directed traffic as their guests filled their plates and took them outside to the picnic tables.

Pennie picked the biggest burger on the plate, winked at Julie and pointed to her plate. Ah yes, revenge tasted sweet and juicy.

TWENTY-NINE

Any time the kids were playing outside, Julie was always on the lookout for squirrels, chipmunks, deer or any wildlife for that matter. She would often ask God to let one of His little critters come to her.

Picking berries in the summer was something the girls always looked forward to. Julie would check on the wild raspberry bushes along the lane, and when the green berries began to appear, she would get so excited, not to mention impatient, for them to ripen. One early summer day when she saw some red and purple beginning to show on the bushes near the barn, she asked if she could take Karen to pick berries on the lane. Their mom gave them each a Cool Whip container into which they could put the berries.

"Remember to be careful of the thorns," she warned. "If you don't eat them all and bring some home, we can start our stash for making raspberry jelly." It was everyone's favorite.

They were perusing the berry bushes on the bank when Julie spotted a little furry animal alongside the road. When she moved closer, she saw its stripes and recognized it was a chipmunk. She walked slowly toward it and it did not run. Did it see her? Then, he actually scampered in her direction. She stepped closer and stooped down. He did not run.

She began to woo him with a soft, high voice, "Come here little chipmunk, it's okay, c'mere…"

She reached out to touch the creature and it backed away but still did not flee. Upon closer examination, she saw his little eyes were shut. He could not see. He was just a baby. Maybe he was like the barn cats' kittens when they were first born and his eyes had not yet opened.

Karen was used to Julie lagging behind. When she turned around to say something to her, she saw Julie crouched down occupied by something on the ground. She was just going to keep going until Julie called her. "Karen, come quick. Look."

Her curiosity made her retrace her steps. "What is it?"

"Look, it's the cutest little thing; he came right to me. His eyes are shut. But I think he came to my voice."

"Aww, he is so cute. But I don't know if you should pick him up."

Julie reached out ever so carefully, "He walked right up to me. Trust me, this is between me and God."

"You and God?" Karen thought about it, but did not understand. "What about Mom? What will she say? Are you taking him home?"

"Why, yes I am. He's mine to take care of now." Julie picked him up and carried him home.

Julie thought he was the cutest thing she had ever seen; only Betty was not so enamored.

"You can't bring that thing in the house," Betty insisted. "Take him back to the woods."

"But Mom, he can't see. I think he got lost from his mom and God wants me to take care of him."

Her dad showed up in time to save the day. "I don't know how long he will make it without his mom, but we can give it a try," Paul encouraged his daughter.

Not so inconspicuously, Betty was giving him *the look*, but he knew how to talk her into things when he wanted to, look or no look.

"Julie, he will be your responsibility. And you'll have to give him a name." He winked at an unhappy Betty.

"Chippy," Julie declared. "His name will be Chippy."

"All right, Chippy it is," said Dad. "Let's find a box and you can get an old towel from the garage. We'll get an eye dropper and see if he'll take a little milk."

Julie took care of Chippy day and night, as long as she was home. However, life did go on and there were times she had to leave him. One Sunday evening when she needed to go to the church for an activity before the service, she gave Karen the responsibility of feeding Chippy with the eye dropper.

When Karen came with their parents for the evening service, she looked nervous as she walked up to Julie and said, "Chippy didn't make it."

"What?" said Julie. "Didn't make it to church? I knew Mom wouldn't let you bring him."

"No...uh, he didn't make it as in he stopped breathing and went to heaven," said Karen with tears welling up in her eyes.

"No! Please tell me that's not true! What happened?"

"I was feeding him with the dropper just like you showed me and he just choked a little and that was it. He didn't move anymore after that."

"You killed him! You gave him too much at one time."

Karen cried harder, not sure if she might have killed him or not. Julie was more upset than she was allowed to show at church, so she pushed back the tears and knew she was going to have a conversation with God about this. She could not think of anything but getting home to check on Chippy to see if it was true. Maybe he was just tired and fell asleep while he was eating.

Bonnie and Gail stayed after church for YAC, Youth After Church. Glenn offered to give them a ride home when they were done. As for the other four Nevels, it was not a pleasant drive home as Julie let the tears flow and gave Karen the cold shoulder.

Betty attempted to soften the blow and said, "It wasn't your sister's fault now, Julie. She loved Chippy, too. He wasn't meant to live in a house. You would've had to let him go in the woods at some point."

Paul tried to comfort her. "Yes, and his eyes never did open so he wouldn't have lived as long as he did without you. You took such good care of him and did just what God asked you to do. You probably spared him from being eaten by a raccoon or hawk or even one of the barn cats."

"Ooo that would be awful!" Julie sobbed.

Paul looked at Betty and shrugged his shoulders. "Guess that was a poor attempt to make her feel better."

Later at home, they had a little funeral for Chippy in a field close to the woods. Betty recited a poem she learned as a child:

> All things bright and beautiful,
> All creatures great and small,
> All things wise and wonderful:
> The Lord God made them all.

Paul read a Scripture about God knowing and caring about when a sparrow falls. Then he sang a verse and chorus of the hymn "His Eye is on the Sparrow." Julie wiped away a tear for Chippy and thought maybe she would pray that a sparrow would befriend her next.

THIRTY

Life was good for the Nevel family. Asbury Lane was the center of family life and a place they willingly shared with friends and family.

Their relationships with the old Army buddies and Army wives, the Sharffs and Sengs, continued as both families grew. There were visits back and forth and even vacations and holidays together. Harry and Ann had three girls by the names of Cheryl, Linda and Holly who were close to the ages of Bonnie, Gail and Julie. Dale and Elaine had not yet been able to have children, so they took on the noble task of being foster parents and offered a loving home to many children who came and went. They were able to adopt twin boys Don and Jeff and daughter Ann. The couples' children became friends and pen pals and considered one another to be part of one big happy family.

Well, happy for the most part. Bonnie, Gail, Cheryl and Linda were a pretty tight-knit group when they got together, leaving the younger Julie and Holly feeling left out. The older girls had a favorite make-believe scenario they would play. It was not the typical playing house, hide-n-seek, board games or Barbies. No, indeed, it was their very own creation; they played "Bank." Using play money from Monopoly and coins from their own piggy banks, they had tellers and customers, telephones, calculators and file boxes. They were quite creative and even had a jingle, tune and all, for their one-of-a-kind bank. They would pleasantly answer the phones singing their jingle, "This is the National H Bank, may we help you sir or ma'am?"

When the Sharffs were visiting the Nevels at the farm, Julie and Holly had plenty of space to go and create their own fun. But still, the idea of being left out by the bigger kids did not sit well with them. Therefore, they would sneak around and devise plans to get in on the bank action. Perhaps they could become famous bank robbers, or at least ruin some of their big sisters' fun. It would usually end up with the older girls yelling, "Mom!" to scare the younger ones off and thwart their plans.

When the Nevels were visiting the Sharffs, the oldest four continued their banking, picking up where they left off from the last visit. While the farm gave them room to run, the Sharffs had some fascinating things at their house, like Harry's drum set and the family's player piano. Gail fell in love with the drums and asked Harry to show her some tricks with the sticks. She dreamed of being a real drummer someday. Harry would load a piano roll onto the spool box, sit down on the piano bench and start pumping the foot pedals. This would cause the perforated roll to turn and the music would begin to play. The beautiful arrangement of "Moon River" was always a request, as well as the song "You'll Never Walk Alone."

Sometimes all three families would gather at one of the homes in a sort of family get-together. The couples appreciated and valued the unique friendship God had granted them and passed the appreciation along to their children. Not to be minimized, these were lifelong friendships bound by common values of faith and patriotism, all stemming from three men from different cities in Pennsylvania being drafted into the Army during the Korean War. People speak of marriages made in heaven; these were indeed friendships made in heaven.

The house on Asbury Lane was built with purpose. Paul had his dream of what it should look like and it poured from him during the building process.

One of the couple's favorite delights at the end of a long day was to sit on the porch in the quiet of the night when the kids were in bed and gaze up at the beautiful night sky. In the country, without the clutter of city lights, it was a wondrous and awesome sight.

"You know what I'm thinking, Betty," Paul said on one frosty but mild March evening.

She glanced over with an mischievous smile. "Despite the male myth that women can read their husband's thoughts, I actually have no idea what you are thinking."

Turning back to the stars, she pretended to admire the view.

Paul sighed.

Finally, she looked back at him, "What are you thinking, my love?"

"I was considering the story of Abraham and how God showed him the heavens and told him that his descendants would outnumber the stars," said Paul, his voice had that dreamy quality his wife knew well. He was content. "God has blessed us beyond the stars He showed to Abraham. We could not begin to count all He has done for us."

"Have I ever thanked you for allowing me to share in those blessings?" she asked.

This time, Paul gazed at the sky and did not respond as though he had not heard her.

She saw the glint in his eyes and knew he was playing with her. She nudged him with her shoulder, "Thank you."

"Thank you," he responded. "Thank you for being my wife. For giving me four wonderful girls. For making this house a home."

For a moment, they took in the night and individually praised God for His faithfulness.

"You know," Paul said softly, "I cannot imagine how God could bless me anymore than He has."

In March of 1971, Betty was looking forward to the end of snow season and signs of spring coming back to the farm. She loved taking walks and getting the girls outside in the fresh air. But this March she felt different. She was not feeling well and just could not quite put her finger on what was wrong. Then the nausea hit and she just did not feel like eating. One day she asked her mother to spend the day with the girls so she could rest. She was exhausted and it was hard keeping up with them. Paul was surprised to come home from work and find her in bed, which was very uncharacteristic of her. He sat down on the edge of the bed when he saw she was awake.

"I hear you had a rough day," he said. "Do you think you have the flu? Maybe I should call the doctor."

"I don't know, maybe. I just feel nauseous and had to fight it all day."

"Well, you rest," he said. "Your mother made supper and we have things under control."

He kissed her and left. It was wonderful to have a husband she could count on. She determined to sleep hoping tomorrow would be better.

But it was not. Over the next few days she still did not feel much better, though it would come and go. The thought crossed her mind that the feeling was similar to those old morning sickness days, but, no... Surely she could not be pregnant. All of the girls were in school now, and she was glad to not be changing diapers anymore. It was going on five years since Karen was born and she was closing in on 40, no longer a spring chicken. Even though they had hoped for a boy, God saw fit to give them four girls and they were content and happy with those little blessings; most of the time. A few more days passed and the nausea was not going away. A trip to the doctor was in order.

The doctor did a general physical and asked some questions.

"Hmm...Could you be pregnant?" he asked.

No, Betty was tempted to say. Instead, she said, "Well I suppose it's possible, but unlikely as we were certain we were done having children. It sure would be a shock."

After some careful thought and another review of the chart, he recommended they check.

The test results came back positive. The Nevels were going to have a fifth child. Betty's first thought after the initial shock was, "Oh no, I'm going to be sick for nine months." Paul's was, "Oh no, another mouth to feed."

That evening Paul asked the girls to come into the living room. Betty was lying on the couch. The two oldest girls were especially afraid something was terribly wrong, as they knew their mom had not been feeling well. It was six years since Aunt Marlene had died, yet they remembered how she was sick first, and then everyone was sad.

"Well, girls, we found out why your mother has been sick." He looked into their curious eyes. "You're going to have another sister or a brother. Your mom is going to have a baby!"

Fear turned to surprise and surprise to excitement as the news dawned on the girls.

"Huh? Really, Mom?" Gail tried to comprehend. Pregnant women were supposed to be happy and glowing. "Why do you have to be sick? Are you doing it right?"

"That's just how my body reacts, unfortunately," her mother attempted to explain, "I was sick with everyone of you."

Julie and Karen thought it was really fun news and giggled with glee. Then the four girls jumped up and down, clapped their hands and danced around the room.

The concerns lingered while Betty suffered through morning, noon and night sickness that changed the routine of the house. They accepted that it was God's will for their family and eventually the doubt became feelings of jubilant anticipation.

Their relatives and church friends were surprised to hear the news. Everyone was saying perhaps they would finally get a boy. Their good friends the Jones had five girls and some teased them that they were just trying to keep up with the Joneses.

In his spare time, Betty had her husband pull out all the girls' old clothes and she sorted through them. He also found a box of cloth diapers and the safety pins to go with them.

It was a good time for Betty to bring up something about which she had wanted to ask her husband. It was the big question of expectant couples of that era. "Honey, have you seen the commercials for the new disposable diapers? Do you know how nice it would be to change a diaper and just throw it away? I can hardly imagine it."

"Uh, yes but don't you think that would get expensive?" It was the response she expected from her frugal husband, yet not the one she wanted to hear. "As far as cloth diapers go, we wouldn't have to buy anything, by the looks of how many are in this box."

Still, Betty persisted. "I know, dear, but think about what we'd save on the water bill. And sometimes you pay for convenience, you know. It would free up some laundry time for me. I want to at least try a few and see how well they work."

Paul reluctantly agreed. "I know it would be easier for you. I wonder how well they really absorb. I say we still hold on to the cloth diapers until we see how it goes."

The crib was set up in the master bedroom in anticipation of the sleepless nights to come.

Summer was miserable for Betty with the heat and the nausea combined. Household air conditioners had become more popular in the past decade, but with the changing seasons in Pennsylvania, they were not seen as a necessity. When fall's cool breezes began to gently blow away summer's humidity, they brought relief and a welcomed change.

It was time for school to start again. Betty had not imagined that she would be sending fifteen-year-old Bonnie off to her sophomore year in high school, with baby number five on the way! Gail at thirteen was at last a teenager, not soon enough for her liking. Julie was eight and going into third grade, while Karen was starting her first school experience with half days in kindergarten.

For a mother pregnant for the fifth time, baby showers were a thing of the past. Some of their friends still gave gifts to help prepare them for this unexpected blessing. Knowing that Paul had agreed to give disposable diapers a try, Judy thought they would be just the perfect gift. In fact, she and her husband bought them a whole case of Pampers.

The big day arrived at the end of November. Paul left the girls with Gram and raced down Asbury Lane with Betty to the Altoona Hospital.

Once again, he was back in the familiar waiting room with a bunch of new fathers who reminded him of the first day of boot camp, only he was the grizzled older drill sergeant who knew what these poor recruits were in for over the next few days, perhaps years. Even though he tried to give the air of confidence, he was apprehensive about what his wife was experiencing somewhere else in the hospital.

One by one, the expectant fathers became fathers and there he was, still; new year, same song.

The nurse finally entered with, "Mr. Nevel?"

"Right here," he said and waited for those all too familiar words.

"It's a boy!" she smiled.

"That's great…" He paused. What had she said? "I'm sorry?"

"A boy, Mr. Nevel. You have a healthy baby boy."

Walking down the hallway to Betty's room, Paul tried to digest the information. Had he heard her correctly? No…

But when he rounded the corner into the room, there was Betty holding a little baby in a blue blanket.

"We have a son, Paul!" she exclaimed.

They wanted to name him after Paul with a different middle name so as not to cause confusion. Therefore a few days later, Paul Jay was introduced to the world as Jay and taken home to Asbury Lane to meet his four older sisters. The girls could hardly wait to hold him, play with him and spoil him.

From one love story came five precious lives. They all grew and learned to love Jesus and learned to love life. It never occurred to them to ever ask why they got to live in such a magical place, though they learned to appreciate it more and more through the years. And flowing out of them came a host of other stories of life and of love.

But those are tales for another time from that special piece of heaven on earth called Asbury Lane…

"On earth there is no heaven, but there are pieces of it."
Jules Renard

ABOUT THE AUTHOR

Julie Nevel is an independent contemporary Christian recording artist based in the Harrisburg area of Pennsylvania. June of 2016 marked 28 years of Julie ministering full-time throughout the U.S. and abroad as a worship leader, singer/songwriter, speaker, concert artist and pianist. In an array of venues, from churches, music festivals and conventions, to prisons, foreign and inner city missions, VBS, retreats, camps and even your neighborhood coffee house, Julie's powerful music ministry captures listeners with original songs written from the heart and reflecting her own personal experiences.

Julie has recorded many projects of her original music throughout her years of ministry. Her most recent CD, Just Show Up, was preceded by Hope for Your Heart, and a children's project, Deep Down in My Heart. Her craft of songwriting has opened doors of opportunity for Julie to write for some special projects. These include the song "The Spirit of the Flame," inspired by the athletes of the Special Olympics and sung at the World Games, and "Step by Step," a song penned for breast cancer awareness and performed for "Making Strides Against Breast Cancer," and many other walks and events. In addition to her songwriting, Julie has written a book, Asbury Lane. She is the founder of the Sister to Sister Women's Conference, which she coordinates and takes to various churches and venues.

Whether leading people to God's throne in praise and worship, or in a concert setting, Julie guides people down a path of adventure that ends deep within the heart. Her music inspires and encourages us, challenging us toward greater depths of faith, and reminding us of the hope we can find through God's amazing love and grace.

www.julienevel.com

NEW BOOKS
COMING SOON
in the Asbury Lane Series

Made in the USA
Middletown, DE
30 March 2022